The View from Split Rock

THE VIEW
FROM
SPLIT
ROCK

A Lighthouse Keeper's Life

Lee Radzak with Curt Brown

MINNESOTA
HISTORICAL
SOCIETY PRESS

The publication of this book was supported through a generous grant from the Dale S. and Elizabeth D. Hanson Fund for Swedish American History.

Front cover: *Christian Dalbec*
Frontispiece: September 2019. *Nathan Klok Photography*

Many spectacular images may also be found at the websites of these fine North Shore photographers, whose work is featured in this book.
Photos p. ii, vii © 2019, 2020 Nathan Klok, https://www.nklokphoto.com
Photo p. 2 © 2020 Hayes Scriven, https://hayesscriven.smugmug.com
Photos p. 7, 42 © 2015, 2009, Dennis O'Hara, https://www.northernimages.com
Photo p. 10 © Nicholas J. Narog, https://nicholasjnarogphotography.pixieset.com
Photo p. 79 © 2013 Paul Sundberg, https://www.paulsundbergphotography.com
Photo p. 111 © 2019 Christian Dalbec, https://www.christiandalbecphotography.com

Map p. 8–9 by Adam Demers
Map p. 14 MNHS

Design: Adam Demers

mnhspress.org

The Minnesota Historical Society Press is a member of the Association of University Presses.

Manufactured in the United States of America

10 9 8 7 6 5 4 3 2 1

International Standard Book Number
ISBN: 978-1-68134-180-4 (paper)
ISBN: 978-1-68134-206-1 (e-book)

Library of Congress Control Number: 2021930042

This and other Minnesota Historical Society Press books are available from popular e-book vendors.

Contents

≈ *Foreword* ≈

He watches the movement of the sun, moon, and stars with the calm, steady demeanor of a lighthouse keeper.

If that sounds like the first line of a romance novel, so be it. It's only fitting, because my husband, Lee Radzak, actually served as a light keeper for thirty-six years. Granted, by the time he took over Split Rock Lighthouse on Lake Superior's craggy North Shore, the lighthouse had been decommissioned for fourteen years. Still, as site manager at the popular historic site, run by the Minnesota Historical Society, Lee carried on the legacy of light keepers at Split Rock dating back more than a century.

This book is his story of those years. It's organized by seasons—our lives were ruled by the seasons—and it's also something of a scrapbook, touching on history, weather, the neighborhood, our family, interactions with the state park, and even the story of catching a bear while in a bathrobe.

Lee's experience as a young man in the Marine Corps taught him discipline and duty. Six years as an archaeologist honed his skills of observing and documenting. He can repair almost anything. I often asked Lee how he knew how to fix furnaces, wire lights, repair a tractor, or calmly deal with major septic issues (I'll spare you the details). There were no people to ask or YouTube videos to watch. His invariable response was to smile and shrug and say, "I'm flying by the seat of my pants, honey."

Our family soon grew to include our children, John and Anna. Each of us was well suited to live in the solid brick house on that isolated cliff, perched high above icy Lake Superior. We are a quiet, easygoing little bunch, so we would probably be a tight-knit family anyway, but living at a remote lighthouse, no doubt, helped forge our solid bond as we rode out storms and hunkered down when the power went out. We kept a close eye on the weather, just as the keepers did in earlier days. We watched storms build for two days and linger for two more after their intensity peaked. We listened to the roar of that enormous body of water below as storm windows blew off in the raging wind.

Oddly enough, those stormy spells didn't frighten us at all. We were content in one another's company and exhilarated by the power of the world around us. We shared a life of blizzards, thunderstorms, starry nights, breathtaking sunrises and sunsets, inside jokes, and easy companionship.

Lee had a long list of responsibilities and relationships to manage: our family, the site's buildings and security, the visitors, the Minnesota Historical Society's administrators, the partners at the Minnesota Department of Natural Resources, the North Shore community, the international historic lighthouse community, and whatever else might come up in a typical workday. In thirty-six years of frozen septic mounds, lightning strikes, belligerent bears, and angry tourists, I never saw him lose his temper. Not once. But one day—November 10, 1985—really confirmed my belief that Lee has the soul of a light keeper. On that same day in 1975, twenty-nine sailors perished when the ore-carrying SS *Edmund Fitzgerald* went down in a storm. Lee turned that sad anniversary into a personal tribute to the lost crew members. A bell-ringing memorial ceremony every November 10 has become a major event, drawing hundreds of visitors every year despite often abysmal November weather. But the *Fitz* memorial began as a solo observance, when this quiet, unassuming man paused to light the retired beacon in honor of the sailors who had passed his lighthouse.

Our family of four is ordinary in many ways, but we were granted the rare privilege to live in an extraordinary place—and we always knew it. It doesn't get better than that.

Jane Radzak

Jane, John, Anna, and
Lee Radzak, with Shamus,
October 2016

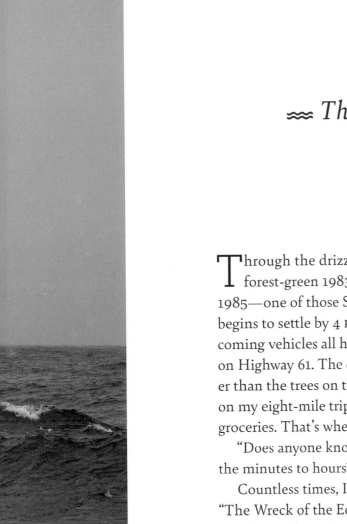

November 2020.
Hayes Scriven

≈ The Gales of November ≈ Came Early

Through the drizzle and fog, I could barely see the lake from my forest-green 1983 Ford Ranger pickup truck. It was November 10, 1985—one of those Sunday afternoons in late autumn when darkness begins to settle by 4 PM along the North Shore of Lake Superior. The oncoming vehicles all had their headlights blazing as they whizzed past me on Highway 61. The clouds, hanging like gray flannel, weren't much higher than the trees on the ridgetops above the lake. I was driving southwest on my eight-mile trip home from Silver Bay, where I'd picked up a few groceries. That's when a familiar song began to play on my truck radio.

"Does anyone know where the love of God goes, when the waves turn the minutes to hours?"

Countless times, I'd heard Gordon Lightfoot sing his popular ballad, "The Wreck of the Edmund Fitzgerald." But this time was different. This was the tenth anniversary of Lake Superior's most infamous shipwreck.

The *Big Fitz,* as twenty-nine crew members called their 729-foot iron ore carrier, mysteriously plunged to the eastern lake bottom during a vicious gale in 1975. When it came to rest 530 feet down, the SS *Edmund Fitzgerald* joined more than three hundred shipwrecks littering Lake Superior's floor. Despite an intensive years-long investigation by the US Coast Guard and the National Transportation Safety Board, the wreck's cause has never been fully explained.

As I steered through the sleet, listening to Gordon Lightfoot in my warm pickup, my mind turned to the *Fitz*'s crew members who had crossed the same water now barely visible through misty rain a decade later. The massive ore boat had sailed out of the Superior, Wisconsin, ore dock, twenty miles down the shore, and past Split Rock Lighthouse during the late afternoon of November 9, 1975—before the weather turned bitter. I thought about the terror they must have felt in their last minutes above that freezing water.

The SS *Edmund Fitzgerald* in the St. Mary's River, about 1975. Robert Campbell

I'd been hired by the Minnesota Historical Society three years earlier, in 1982, to be site manager for Split Rock Lighthouse—the iconic, decommissioned light station built after a wicked gale in 1905. On its rocky cliff-top perch forty-five miles up the shore from Duluth, the blond-brick lighthouse has become one of the world's most photographed lighthouses and one of Minnesota's top tourist stops. My family made the lighthouse our home for thirty-six years, following the seasonal changes of quiet winter nights overlooking the glass-calm lake to peak summer months of swarming crowds. The largest of the Great Lakes sprawled out our front door, and the lighthouse stood outside our kitchen window.

When I returned to the lighthouse that November night in 1985, my wife, Jane, was fixing supper and wrangling our son, John—then just one year old. "This is the tenth anniversary of the *Fitzgerald*'s sinking," I told her, "and I want to do something special. I'm going to go up to the tower and light the lamp—illuminate the lighthouse beacon to remember the *Fitz* and her crew."

Jane thought shining the light was a wonderful idea. She would hold supper for me. It was nearly dark by the time I walked the fifty yards from our old keeper's house to the lighthouse itself. I unlocked the door, following the beam of my flashlight, and stepped quietly through the passageway from the cleaning room and into the watch room in the base of the lighthouse.

I paused for a deep breath before starting my climb up the thirty-two steps of the spiral staircase that snakes up to the lens room. My steps echoed off the glazed brick walls of the tower. I had climbed these steps hundreds of times alone at night—seldom turning on any of the lower lights in the lighthouse. At night, alone in the tower, I felt a closeness, a strong kinship, to the thirty-five light keepers who once walked these same steps in the dark. The lighthouse was quiet, except for the wind whistling through the windows, the rain spattering on the big curved glass panes of the tower, and my footfalls on the cast-iron stairs.

From the cabinet in the lens room, I removed the same crank handle that all the keepers had used since 1910 to wind up the 180 pounds of cast-iron weights attached to the cable that rotates the lens. As I cranked, I considered how the crew of the *Fitz* must have felt sailing past Split Rock and into the unknown that afternoon in 1975. By then, the lighthouse and its foghorns provided them neither guidance nor solace. The US Coast Guard had taken Split Rock Lighthouse out of service six years earlier, in 1969.

I hoisted the weights up the full 150 cranks, which would give the lens two hours of rotation. Then I flipped the switch that lit the thousand-watt incandescent lamp. The glow filled the inside of the lens and shot out across the lake, illuminating the night. To soak in the full effect, I climbed onto the upper gallery deck, which put me level with the beacon itself. Careful not to look into the powerful beam, I opened the hatch to the outside lantern deck and stepped out into the dark mist. I had to watch my footing—the outer railing of the lantern deck is only knee-high—and I used the bronze handholds anchored into the mulleins of the windows, the same handholds that the keepers used when cleaning the outside of the windows. As I faced the lake, I could hear waves splashing on the rocks nearly two hundred feet below. I could see the lights of an ore carrier about ten miles out on the lake. No doubt they were watching the beacon spilling from Split Rock. I wondered what they thought.

After Split Rock Lighthouse was decommissioned and became a historic site in the 1970s, the Minnesota Historical Society asked the Coast Guard if the beacon could be lit from time to time for ceremonial purposes. Permission was granted if we avoided operating the light on a set schedule upon which ships or small boats might depend. On official Lake Superior navigational charts, Split Rock Light Station is listed as "abandoned." Over the years, I've asked ore carrier captains that travel past Split Rock if they are at all confused or curious about the rare times when they do see Split Rock lit at night. They shrug and say that they know it's historic. They enjoy when it's lit, but they don't pay it much attention. One captain replied that with all the radar, GPS, and other modern navigational equipment now on the bridge of the Great Lakes freighters, he's lucky if he can get his crew to look out the windows.

Back on that night in 1985, I walked around the outside lantern deck and stood in front of the large curved windows with the light at my back. With each rotation, as the beam swept from left to right along the horizon, the bright light hit me from behind and threw my gargantuan shadow out across Lake Superior. There is little heat generated from the light passing through the prisms, but the bright glow gave me the illusion of warmth from the lens at my back. The sweeping of the beam and my huge shadow moving out on the lake gave me a dizzy feeling. All I could see was the light of the beam hitting the mist out into infinity, my dark shadow, and then the surrounding darkness as the lens rotated behind me. I gripped the handholds tightly. I stayed out there until my fingers grew numb.

I carefully climbed back down to the lens room floor and retraced my steps down through the tower—locking up the lighthouse and walking the seventy-five paces home to a warm dinner. Nearly two hours later, before the weights rotating the lens hit bottom and needed rewinding, I climbed back up into the lens room and switched off the beacon.

Lighting the lamp on the tenth anniversary was simply a symbolic way to honor the crew of the *Edmund Fitzgerald*—a gesture I thought no one would notice. But a few people along the shore wondered what was happening, and in the days that followed, I heard from them. Our closest neighbor, who lived about a mile away, asked me why it was on. Others in Silver Bay were driving past when the light was lit and stopped by to ask about it. One of the summer tour guides who worked at Split Rock, Ed

Maki Jr., called from Silver Bay. His father-in-law, Nolan Church, was a crew member who went down with the *Fitz.*

Everyone agreed that illuminating the beacon was a fine way to commemorate the *Edmund Fitzgerald.* The next year, in 1986, I invited some of these people to watch when I lit it up again on November 10. A few more folks showed up in 1987 when I lit it for the twelfth anniversary of the sinking. The early gatherings were informal, and I couldn't allow people inside the tower after dark because of safety concerns. Crowds continued to grow until a few dozen visitors stopped by each November 10 for the ceremonial lighting.

"When the gales of November come early," as Gordon Lightfoot says, the weather can grow cold and windy with rain or snow on November 10. But the crowds kept increasing, so we decided to do something to accommodate them. We didn't charge anything, or even call it an event, for the first five years of our *Fitzgerald* commemorations. By 1990, I secured funding for two tour guides, and—with an exception during the pandemic year of 2020—the visitor center has opened each November 10 for people

The lighthouse beacon, 2012

to see the beacon lit in the evening and to memorialize the crew of the ill-fated *Edmund Fitzgerald.* As the crowds continued to swell, we added even more staff, and we could open the tower after dark for everyone.

To see the beacon lit at night from inside brings the lighthouse to life, showing how the historic clockwork mechanism and lens operate. It enables visitors to walk in the footsteps of the early light keepers.

We began conducting a bell ceremony like the one Gordon Lightfoot sang about: "The church bell chimed till it rang twenty-nine times for each man on the Edmund Fitzgerald." We soon started advertising the lighting ceremony through Minnesota Historical Society press releases to media outlets. This grabbed the attention of a few radio and television stations, who interviewed me and showed up for the beacon lighting. By 1995, on the twentieth anniversary of the Fitzgerald sinking, the event was receiving national news coverage. People began making pilgrimages to Split Rock Light Station from as far away as South Carolina, California, and New England. We were amazed at the intense interest. It grew so popular that, on the twenty-fifth anniversary in 2000, when November 10 fell on a Friday, we decided to hold a two-day ceremony and to light the beacon on Friday and Saturday. More than two thousand people on Friday and another twelve hundred on Saturday visited the lighthouse for the beacon lighting.

My intent was always to avoid a festive atmosphere as we remembered the victims. But as the popularity of the lamp lighting mounted, I really wanted to know why the event was so popular. After all, it was a four-hour drive from the Twin Cities. It was held on November 10, regardless of what day of the week that fell on, and November is always a dicey proposition for long-distance travel to the North Shore. So I began asking visitors. Some wanted to climb the tower and see the beacon lit. Others hoped to see a fall storm kicking up huge waves on Lake Superior. And many possessed a keen interest in the wreck of the *Fitzgerald* and shipwrecks in general. But everyone I talked to said that something deep and meaningful resonates in them during the brief muster of the last watch ceremony, as the beacon lights up the night in memory of the crew of the *Edmund Fitzgerald,* the most famous of the hundreds of Lake Superior shipwrecks.

The lighting ceremony, 2015. *Dennis O'Hara*

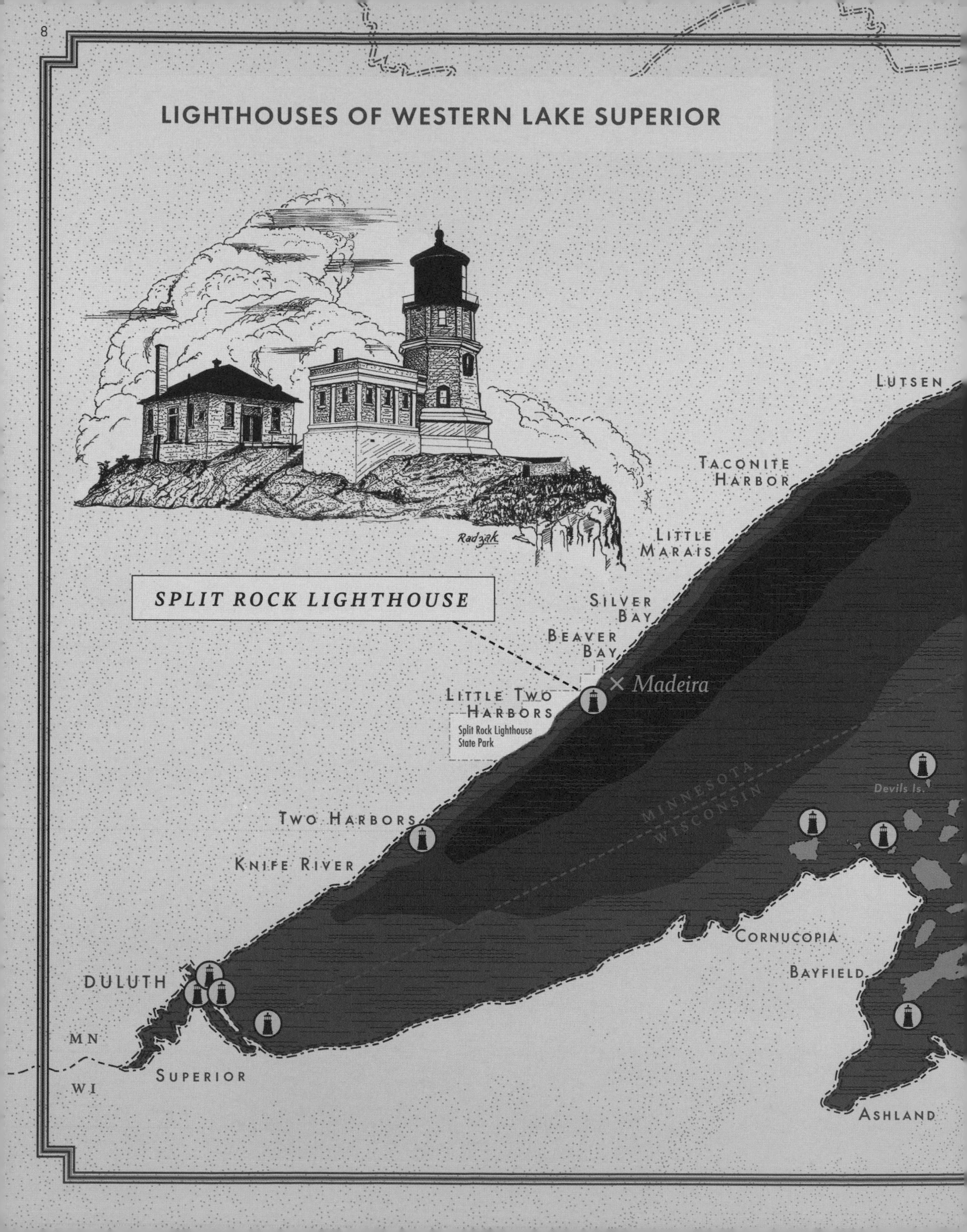

LIGHTHOUSES OF WESTERN LAKE SUPERIOR

Radzak

SPLIT ROCK LIGHTHOUSE

LUTSEN

TACONITE
HARBOR

LITTLE
MARAIS

SILVER
BAY

BEAVER
BAY

× *Madeira*

LITTLE TWO
HARBORS

Split Rock Lighthouse
State Park

Devils Is.

MINNESOTA
WISCONSIN

TWO HARBORS

KNIFE RIVER

CORNUCOPIA

BAYFIELD

DULUTH

MN

WI

SUPERIOR

ASHLAND

CANADA

U.S.

GRAND
PORTAGE
RESERVA-
TION

ISLE
ROYALE

GRAND
MARAIS

LAKE

SUPERIOR

WISCONSIN
MICHIGAN

Outer Is.

APOSTLE
ISLANDS

MI
WI

0 2 4 6 8 10
MILES

1.

≋ *Autumn* ≋

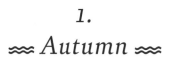

On a dark Halloween afternoon in 1982, we packed up our belongings from our apartment in Bloomington, Minnesota—a suburb of Minneapolis—and headed north to Split Rock Lighthouse. I squinted through snow flurries while navigating the dark curves of Highway 61 and worrying that deer might cross the road at any moment. The dark stretch of highway was all but void of traffic. We zoomed past Gooseberry Falls State Park, then past the old Twin Points Resort on the right, and then Split Rock Cabins. As we neared the Split Rock River, I grew giddy with excitement. My brother, Dean, shared the seat of the small, rented U-Haul truck crammed with all of our worldly possessions. Jane followed in her car, accompanied by her brother, Jerry, and his wife, Mollie. As we crossed the Split Rock River, we drove through what would soon become developed as Split Rock Lighthouse State Park. The truck's headlights pushed a cone of light ahead of us, illuminating the pitch-black forest on either side as we turned off toward the lighthouse a couple of miles northeast of the river. We spied a tiny cabin at the top of the hill on the state park entrance road. The Minnesota Department of Natural Resources contact station building was, back then, the only DNR presence in the fledgling, undeveloped state park. We passed it and drove on to our new home: Dwelling No. 2, the middle of three keepers' houses.

That first fall, as we settled in, I began my duties as site manager for the Minnesota Historical Society, which owns and operates the lighthouse in trust for the people of Minnesota. I had already spent six years working for the society as an archaeologist, and this was a major change in responsibilities. Marching orders for my new job were wide and varied, and I loved the idea of the variety and challenge—and the independence of being two hundred miles from headquarters. I was to manage all aspects of protecting the historic site and to provide and expand on ways to share the story

The keepers' dwellings, 2013. The Minnesota Historical Society restored Dwelling No. 1, at front, for tours. We lived in the middle house, and the third was used for office space, then storage.

~~~~~~~~~~~~~~~~~~~~

OPPOSITE: Split Rock from Day Hill, 2014

of the lighthouse and keepers. I was expected to provide security, develop a tour program, hire and oversee a staff of interpreters, provide a safe experience for visitors, maintain the grounds and buildings in their historic appearance, be a local representative of the Minnesota Historical Society, and, last but not least, live in the middle of the three light keepers' homes, year-round.

During off-hours, Jane and I began to eagerly explore the miles of shoreline and forest surrounding us. On snowshoes and cross-country skis, we tromped and glided through snow disturbed only by deer, coyote, and wolf tracks. In the days before the DNR began laying out its state park trails, we were free to travel the path of least resistance or most fun. Within a decade, this place would become a popular state park. But in the first years, the shoreline saw almost no human traffic, with the only visitors heading straight to the lighthouse. I was to learn that autumn, like spring, is fleeting on the North Shore. Winter is the nine-hundred-pound gorilla of seasons, and summer is like an oasis on the journey through the year—a short, inviting stop on a long trip. At Split Rock, you feel summer sliding away by the first or second week of August. The sun rises later, and the morning air turns brisk. By late August, some of the leaves on the birch trees are already showing ominous signs of color change from green to brassy yellow. The sun rides lower over the lake every day, and I watched the shadow of the lighthouse lengthen and stretch across the lawn at midday. Labor Day weekend marks the turning point, when the fall transition picks up speed. If I had to slot a North Shore autumn on the calendar, I would place it in September and October. By early November, winter has gained a firm foothold as each new snow squall pushes the last of the migrating birds south. I gazed to the southwest as the sun set a little farther to the south, a couple of minutes earlier each day. By November, the sun sets behind Day Hill, casting the lighthouse in shadow by 4:30 PM.

~~~

Tram house and
tramway ruins

Boathouse
and dock
site

trail to lake and state park

stairway to lake

old tramway

Houses and storage barns

Visitor Center

Oilhouse

Lighthouse

Fog signal
building

Hoist and
derrick
ruins

A TOUR OF THE SITE

Split Rock Lighthouse, my new home and workplace,
is a premier example of an intact early-twentieth-century
Great Lakes light station. Built in response to a fierce storm that
lashed western Lake Superior and sank or damaged twenty-nine
ships in November 1905, it served from 1910 until 1969. The US
government determined that a lighthouse along the North Shore "in the
vicinity of Split Rock, Minnesota" would be the best solution for protecting shipping, and in 1908 it purchased 7.6 acres atop the cliff for $200. A
federal allocation of $75,000 was made to the US Lighthouse Service to con-
struct the eleven buildings in 1909. Because there were no roads leading to the new light station

site, all 310 tons of building materials had to be delivered by
boat and hauled up the side of the cliff by a hoist and derrick
perched on the cliff edge.

Split Rock was considered a major and important light
station of its time. In addition to the lighthouse (with an
attached cleaning room for supplies for servicing the lens), it
also included a twin foghorn housed in a separate fog signal
building. In foggy weather, three times a minute, its two large
air compressors sent a signal out through the twin copper

megaphones on the roof that could be heard five miles away. Because of the importance of the light and the foghorn, three light keepers staffed the station. They lived with their families near the lighthouse in three identical houses—Dwellings Nos. 1, 2, and 3. A storage barn adjacent to each of the houses held coal and other supplies. The concrete oil house, a structure common to all lighthouses that burned kerosene in their beacons, was built a short distance from the other buildings to store flammable materials. Down a long flight of stairs, a boathouse and dock stood at the shoreline. In 1915, a tramway and cable house were constructed, and the keepers hoisted supplies up the hill in a small cart.

All but two of the original buildings still stand. The boathouse is gone, replaced by a small pump house. The boathouse, deemed obsolete after a road was built to the lighthouse, was burned as surplus property in the 1950s. In 1969, the last year the Coast Guard manned the station, one of the storage barns burned to the ground.

As the saying goes, everybody loves a lighthouse. The State of Minnesota took over the lighthouse in 1970, and the Minnesota Historical Society became responsible for preserving and interpreting the light station beginning in 1976. The stories of those years are told in the "park and site" sections of this book.

OPPOSITE: The derrick hoists construction materials from the steamer *Red Wing*, 1909; construction, about 1909.
ABOVE: Aerial view of the still-active light station, 1959; tram car, 1916. *All photos MNHS*

A FEW YEARS LATER, September meant back to school for our two children, John and Anna (born in 1984 and 1987). They attended school in Silver Bay. The bus picked them up at the curb in the parking lot in front of the visitor center every school day at 7:20 AM. After the kids started school, Jane took a job at the health clinic in Silver Bay, so she was getting ready for work too. That prompted a morning scurry in our household. There was one small bathroom in the old light keeper's house we called home. So we needed to share space as we all prepared for our day. One person combed hair while using the bathroom mirror above the sink and someone else bent over the same sink to brush teeth. Another family member showered in the bathtub while someone else used the toilet. (We always have been a close family). Even with a son and a daughter, it worked out.

In all the years of the school bus picking up the kids, I don't remember the driver, Kenny, ever being late. He was as steady as they come. No matter how deep the snow or how icy the roads, he always managed to get the school bus up the steep road from the highway right on time. At the end of the school day, like clockwork, the yellow bus dropped the kids in front of the visitor center at 3:20 PM. In September, when the weather was still nice and the leaves danced in full color, there were always visitors in the parking lot.

John and Anna wait for the bus, about 1995.

With curious glances, they watched the school bus stop to drop off our kids. Some asked the staff if kids really lived at the lighthouse, and they were often surprised to hear that, like the keepers' kids in the past, they were just normal children living in a special place.

~~~

A peregrine falcon on the lighthouse, 2018

AUTUMN WAS A TIME for wildlife on the move, especially birds. The North Shore is a special place for bird watching during migration time. Most bird species avoid flying directly across Lake Superior; straight south from Split Rock, it's twenty-five miles over open water to Wisconsin's South Shore. They follow the North Shore instead, southwest down to the head of the lake near Duluth, where Hawk Ridge has become a popular spot for birders. Standing with binoculars raised, they watch as the birds funnel down the lake to the estuary of the St. Louis River between Duluth and Superior, Wisconsin.

To me, nighthawks were always the harbinger of autumn. Their appearance over the lighthouse marked the start of the great fall migration, and it always felt too soon. For several days in mid-August, the sky filled with flocks of nighthawks, all keeping about a hundred feet apart with no apparent pattern to their flight as they swooped and dived for what insects they could grab on their way. About a month later, in September, great flocks of loons flew down the shore—individually silent, but part of a great movement that took hours to pass.

We hated to see the hummingbirds leave every fall. Around the first week in September, male hummingbirds began migrating south, leaving the females and young to depart by mid-September. The feeders at our windows that fed dozens of hummers all summer suddenly grew quiet, and we took them down. It always amazed us to think that these tiny birds could fly thousands of miles to spend the winters in Central America and even South America.

By late September, the peregrine falcon family that nested on the cliff face below the lighthouse all summer left for points south. The ducks and small birds must have breathed a sigh of relief, no longer watching for the falcons diving up to two hundred miles per hour to make them a meal. In late September, most of the yellow and russet fall colors along the North Shore glowed at their peak, with hawk migration in full swing. These raptors also followed the shoreline to avoid crossing the lake. Many of them flew right over the lighthouse. A few times I was lucky enough to look straight up to see a kettle of hundreds of hawks circling tightly on the rising thermal air currents high above the lighthouse. I always made sure to share this amazing display with lighthouse visitors. It was a rare and special sight.

Various birds and animals visited our crabapple tree at this time of year. In the yard near the keepers' dwellings, planted between two storage barns by an unnamed keeper, a beautiful crabapple tree had grown for more than seventy years—producing bushels of crabapples every year. As soon as the apples ripened in early September, they were easy picking for cedar waxwings and ruffed grouse. Several of the grouse made their homes around the lighthouse, and we often saw four or five of them picking fruit. All our dogs (we had four, over the years) loved to hunt grouse with me in the fall, across the highway and into the hills. But the dogs learned to accept the grouse in the yard and mostly ignored them. Some years, a bear, usually alone, feasted on these apples to fatten up before winter hibernation. It was a scene straight out of a cartoon: the bear comfortably parked its rear end high up in the tree on one branch, while gathering other branches loaded with apples and delicately picking them off, one by one. Naturally, our golden retriever, Captain, wasn't happy to discover that a bear had slipped into his yard. He sat under the tree and watched every move that bear made. We eventually brought him into the house to let the bear climb down, waddle across the yard, and hop the chain-link fence with a belly full of crabapples. The fruit was also a favorite of our dogs, who ate up any strays that hit the driveway. Shamus, our yellow Lab, needed to have several teeth pulled in his later years. The vet said that it was likely the result of the sugars in the crabapples he had chewed.

LOGBOOKS

Keeping daily logbooks was among the head light keeper's primary tasks. Today, these written legacies give us a bare-bones glimpse of life atop Split Rock. The writers included two head keepers at Split Rock under the US Lighthouse Service from 1910 through 1939, and three more men who served when the US Coast Guard replaced the Lighthouse Service in 1940. Their daily logs recorded weather conditions, keepers' health, lighthouse visitors, maintenance tasks, equipment problems, and unusual happenings.

The content and writing style in these handwritten journals varied considerably from keeper to keeper. For instance, the logbook entries of the first keeper at Split Rock, Orren "Pete" Young, were short, almost curt. Many of his daily notes consisted of simply, "General duties at station." He reserved his more elaborate entries for unusual occurrences, like when supply tender boats visited.

Luckily for us, the first assistant keeper from 1913 to 1923, Harry Thompson, kept his own, more colorful diary, noting everything from hunting and fishing trips to the Split Rock River to drunken nights with laborers building the tramway. Thompson's journal enhances our understanding of the early years at the light station. A large, good-natured man, Thompson was also a great storyteller. He

subscribed to several newspapers and visited often with the fishermen living less than a mile from the lighthouse in Little Two Harbors Cove. His diary elaborated on the comings and goings of friends and relatives of the three keepers at the light station and what they ate. He chronicled invitations to the fishermen's camp to share a keg of beer and recorded their success with their nets.

While Head Keeper Young's official light station logbook entries provide a representative picture of lighthouse routine, First Assistant Thompson's journal for the same days gives us a clearer picture of the lifestyle of these early years at Split Rock. He talked about such typical events as how Lighthouse Service tenders *Amaranth* and *Marigold* resupplied the light station. He tracked loans he gave to other keepers—and when he got paid back—and noted four broken record cylinders when his mail-order Victrola arrived.

Thompson was an avid reader and kept current newspaper subscriptions that were delivered on the supply boats. In his journal, Thompson talked about events happening in the larger world beyond the lighthouse. In his entry for September 10, 1918, he mentioned that week's bombing of the federal building in downtown Chicago that killed four people. In a lengthy entry for October 17, 1918, he

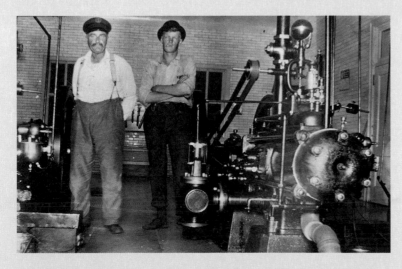

ABOVE: Keeper Harry Thompson and Conrad Lorntson of Beaver Bay in the fog signal building, in a photo taken by keeper Lee Benton in 1911. *Split Rock Lighthouse research files* RIGHT: Keeper Orren "Pete" Young, July 1926. MNHS

mentioned the influenza outbreak killing hundreds of soldiers and that week's deadly forest fire around Moose Lake and Cloquet. Home Guard troops dug mass graves after the October 12 fire, the state's worst-ever natural disaster with more than 450 people killed. Nearly a month later,

Keeper Franklin Covell and his family, 1942. *MNHS*

on November 12, Thompson's words captured history, albeit with misspellings: "The Armistice was signed by Germany Austria Hungaria Turkey 9 AM o'clock the war practicaly setteled. their was great rejoycing all over America. Woodrow Wilson president second term." Thompson served at Split Rock through 1923, then continued his career at other lighthouses on Lake Superior.

When Pete Young retired as head keeper in 1928, first assistant keeper Franklin Covell, who succeeded Thompson, took over. In his official logs for the station, Covell offered much more detail than Young had. He focused on the job itself, always stating weather conditions, when the fog-horns were operated, and what maintenance tasks were performed. From time to time, he offered additional tidbits about family life. In August 1929, he wrote that two "airoplanes" passed over the station on a return trip from Port Arthur, Ontario, to Duluth along the new airmail route. This was two years after Charles Lindbergh's transatlantic flight.

Covell detailed how accidents and injuries

befell keepers working alone. On November 7, 1931, he wrote about repairing air compressors high on a ladder in the fog signal building when the ladder slipped from underneath him—dropping him face-first on the concrete floor. He broke two ribs and his nose and bruised his shoulder and the side of his head. Doctors Burns and Monroe were called from Two Harbors. Covell matter-of-factly ended the log entry with the barometric pressure and the day's temperature (two below to eighteen above), noting that the weather is "fine cold south west wind."

By the time I scoured the official logbooks of the early light keepers decades later, the light keepers were long gone. But I felt this was a fine tradition to continue. I knew it was important for me to keep a daily record, given my sometimes faulty memory and all the daily tasks and activities on my site manager's to-do list. Like the keepers of yore, keeping a log would be useful for future reference. So I took time every day to record things that the keepers would have found relevant.

I realized that most of what I wrote each day would be of no future interest to anyone but me. I included details of restoration work on the historic buildings, efforts to maintain the original lens assembly with its mercury float, headaches with tourists trespassing in the middle of the night, celebrities who visited, and storms that blew out power and knocked down trees. Following the example of Harry Thompson, who mentioned his tenth wedding anniversary in 1913, I noted personal family highlights, from bringing our children home after their births at the little hospital in Two Harbors to Anna and John going off to college. When our son proposed to his wife at the base of the lighthouse, I jotted it down in the journal. And I tried to make brief comments about important events beyond the lighthouse, such as September 11, 2001.

Somewhere at Split Rock, probably in the Dwelling No. 3 closet where artifacts are stashed, you might find an old cardboard box holding thirty-seven red hardbound annual journals. I filled each with scribbled handwritten entries, one for each year from 1982 to 2019.

Several mountain ash trees, native to the North Shore, grow on the grounds around the light station. They don't grow very large, but every fall each ash tree produces hundreds of clusters of berries that ripen to a beautiful red-orange color. Large flocks of cedar waxwings descend on each tree and strip off all its berries in a matter of hours. Ruffed grouse love to eat mountain ash berries as well.

Virginia creeper vines grew thick on the four-foot-high chain-link fence that surrounded our yard. To soften up the visual effect of the fence, I began planting the vines in the 1980s. Each year they grew thicker, until they covered the entire fence with a blanket of leaves that turned a beautiful crimson each fall—but only if we managed to keep the white-tail deer from eating the vines down to the ground in the winter. The rest of the year featured enough natural browse in the woods to satisfy their appetites. But as the snow deepened and the weather turned severe, hungry deer were attracted to the vines, and several grazed every night in our yard. I began covering the fence and the vines with deer netting in the fall and removing it in May. It was comical to see the deer try to figure out how to work around the netting to get a taste of the vines. Deer also loved many of the perennial plants that Jane planted in a lovely garden behind the storage barns. Before she convinced me to fence her garden, they especially loved digging up her tulip bulbs.

A ruffed grouse in the crabapple tree, October 2014

BECAUSE WE LIVED where I worked, in housing provided by my employer, I had to develop boundaries between work-related duties and the chores and responsibilities related to our family and our home. I was being paid a salary for, in theory, a forty-hour week. Part of that salary was free rent, provided in exchange for the day-and-night responsibilities of providing security of the site and safety for visitors. Through the winter I was able to mostly keep my workweek to forty hours, but in the frenzied summer and fall season it felt like I was always responding to staff, contractors, and visitors. The work day stretched from sunup to sundown ... and beyond. There was no overtime pay; my employer and I both assumed that you work to get the job done, however long that took.

I always felt that I should do the tasks of maintaining our house and yard on my personal time. It was sometimes difficult to draw a line, though. Do I mow the lawn or put up the storm windows on all three houses on my days off? Or should that be part of my workday? As with the early keepers, the heating bill for the houses was paid by my employer, so it was important to get the storm windows up to save heat all winter. I usually did this work on my days off because I was too busy at other times, and mostly I didn't mind because I was at home with my family.

But every fall, just the thought of putting up those storm windows made me groan. Each of the three keeper's dwellings has seventeen windows. That's fifty-one in all. When the houses were built in 1910, a storm window and a screen window were provided for every one of them. Each of the large storm windows had a wood frame with two twenty-eight-inch-square panes of glass, wavy with age. And around the first of June, I replaced the storm windows with screen windows. On Dwelling No. 1, the restored keeper's house open to the public, I placed screens on six windows and in the two screen doors to give staff and visitors plenty of ventilation on the warmer days of summer. On Dwelling No. 2, our house, I put up screens on eleven of the seventeen windows and on the two doors so that on warm summer days we could open the windows and get the wonderful lake breeze. On Dwelling No. 3, the vacant house farthest from the lighthouse that is used as maintenance and storage for the site, I put up three screens for some air movement. I changed these windows twice a year: storms to screens in the spring and then screens back to storms in the fall. It wasn't until the last several years, when I was in my fifties and sixties, that the site had maintenance staff whom I could ask to change windows on Dwelling No. 1 and Dwelling No. 3. I continued doing this work on our house, though, as I did not feel right asking them to do it. That extension ladder seemed to get longer and those storm windows somehow got heavier every year.

Every fall I picked a calm day, raised an extension ladder to the upper-floor windows, and removed each screen window that had been up since early June. Jane cleaned the outside of the interior window, and I cleaned the inside and outside of the storm window. Then I climbed the ladder again, hauling the five-foot-tall storm window. It was always a thrill to be up on the ladder, especially when I reached the second-floor windows on the lake side of the house. A look back over my shoulder and I could see practically straight down over the cliff to the lake 150 feet below or straight out over the sparkling water to the Apostle Islands thirty miles away. Because of winter storms and high winds at the lighthouse, each storm window needed to be attached to the window frame by four hook-and-eye fasteners inside and four additional outer fasteners. While I held the window in place, Jane latched the inner hook-and-eye fasteners, and I snapped the outer window fasteners.

An annual task: replacing the storm windows, 2018

The view from our bedroom
window, 2014

Despite all these precautions, each winter a major storm usually blew a window off the house. Many people who visit Split Rock Light Station come from the southern United States, places with warm climates and mild winters. When I mentioned changing storm windows, or when they saw me putting them up, they asked why. They had no idea how common it is Up North to put up a second outside window to help keep the cold out and the heat in.

It was always satisfying to get the storm windows in place, but each fall I left one screen window on longer than the others, up until snow threatened. Our bedroom overlooked the lake, and Jane and I loved to fall asleep to the sound of the waves on the rocks below the cliff—or to the occasional howl of a coyote or wolf back in the hills. We were willing to put up with a little chill at night for that pleasure.

Every October, we filled the empty cistern in the basement with fire-wood to last us through the winter. Each of the three keepers' houses had a brick cistern in the basement beneath the kitchen floor. Early on, these were used to hold water for household use. Rainwater was collected from the roofs or lake water was pumped up the hill from Lake Superior and stored in the cisterns. After 1940, when the first well was drilled at the light station, the cisterns were no longer used. Sometime in the 1960s, a Coast Guard keeper stationed in the house cut an opening through the brick lining from the basement into the cistern, just large enough to walk through, making it a perfect place to store firewood.

We lit our wood-burning stove in the basement only during winter power outages or when the oil-burning furnace failed to maintain a comfortable temperature in the house, but the wood was a crucial supplement. Toward the end of each summer, I hired a local logger to deliver a load of birch firewood to our yard. I cut the wood to length and split it. And before the snow started flying, I opened one of the basement windows and set up a wooden plank as a slide to deliver the firewood into the basement. This was a two-person job, so Jane took charge of the woodpile outside. She slid each piece of firewood down the chute with just the right amount of thrust for me to catch it at the bottom and toss the log into the cistern. A few years later our young son, John, proudly took over the job of pushing the wood down the slide.

It gave us great satisfaction and a feeling of snug security to fill the cistern with a cord of firewood to last the coming winter. During the coldest days, we built a fire in the woodstove and warmed the basement, along with the living and dining rooms on the first floor. Our young children lay on the heated living room floor with our dog and played board games in the sun shining in from the windows facing south over Lake Superior.

~~~

Storing firewood with John, about 1990

DOUBLE DROWNING

Our life at the lighthouse seemed idyllic, but there were dangers around us. As the children became more mobile and independent, we had to teach them to stay away from the cliff, be careful near the water, and keep themselves safe as they began their own explorations. Everyone who has lived on the North Shore has needed these skills—lake smarts, respectful attention to the weather, common sense.

The first head light keeper at Split Rock was fifty-two-year-old, longtime sailor Orren "Pete" Young, and he had a great deal of lake experience. His two assistant keepers, Edward Sexton and Roy Gill, did not. And they paid for it with their lives.

They were the first of the thirty-five light keepers who worked at Split Rock through its fifty-nine years of operation. During that first year in 1910, the Split Rock Lumber Company still operated a camp at the mouth of the Split Rock River, about two and a half miles down the shore. Near the lumber camp, a long wharf jutted out into deep water, enabling the steamer *America* to dock there for mail drops when it churned up the North Shore three times a week.

The dock at the lighthouse, used for supply drops from the Lighthouse Service tenders, was short, and the water was too shallow for the *America;* delivering mail there would require launching a skiff and rowing to shore. It was agreed that the keepers could pick up their mail at the logging camp. That first year, the light station had only one small wooden rowboat. It was sixteen feet long, pointed at the bow and stern,

with two seats and two sets of oars, and it had lapped siding, a style often called "clinker-built." The keepers christened the little boat *Clinker.*

Pete Young could sail anything that would float, and he rigged a sail for it, as well as a mast and rudder. He sailed the boat with one hand on the rudder and the other hand holding a line tied to the end of the sail. If a sudden gust of wind came up, he could let the line go. One day he caught one of the assistants in the boat with the sail tied to the seat and he scolded him: *Never, never tie off the sail,* as a quick puff of wind could catch the sail and tip over the boat.

In the early afternoon of Sunday, October 2, 1910, Keeper Young asked Sexton and Gill to take the

HE SPOTTED THE LITTLE BOAT FLOATING ABOUT TWO HUNDRED FEET OFFSHORE, BOTTOM UP.

Clinker to the logging camp to pick up the light station mail. The assistant keepers failed to return by nightfall. Pete knew there was trouble, but he couldn't leave to look for Sexton and Gill. He needed to light the beacon when darkness fell. From sunset to sunrise, he stood all three watches by himself—filling the kerosene,

lighting the lamp, and keeping the weights wound to revolve the lens. At 8 AM the following morning, dead tired from standing watch all night and deeply worried about Gill and Sexton, Young hiked out along the shore toward the Split Rock River. Nearing the logging camp, he spotted the little boat floating about two hundred feet offshore, bottom up. On Monday, October 3, Head Keeper Young entered in the light station daily log: "Keeper left the Station at 8 AM to look for the assts [assistants] and found the boat about two miles from the light afloat bottom up about 20 rods from shore. That shows that both men drowned."

When they towed the boat to shore, Young found the sail still tied off to the seat. The bodies were nowhere to be seen.

As the tragic drownings of the two assistants hit home for Young, he also realized there was work to do. He would need to keep the beacon and foghorns running by himself until replacements for his lost assistants were found. Records don't tell us if Pete Young's wife, Florence, or their three kids—Myrtle, Grace, and Clarence—were at Split Rock that early October. But we do know that Edward Sexton's young, pregnant wife was with him at the lighthouse. It's hard to imagine the heartache this woman suffered, waiting for her husband to return. And think of Pete Young having to inform her when the boat was found along the shore, empty, her husband's body somewhere in the chilly lake water.

While not much is known about second assistant keeper Roy Gill,

The *Clinker,* as photographed by Lee Benton in 1911. *Split Rock Lighthouse research files*

Ed Sexton was part of a lighthouse community. Ed's father, Joseph Sexton, began his Lighthouse Service career in 1886, at age thirty-six, as a second assistant light keeper at the Outer Island Lighthouse in Wisconsin's Apostle Islands. Joseph had married Mary Elizabeth Stahl in 1870, and they had four children while he served at the Outer Island light. Edward Sexton was born in 1884, grew up at a lighthouse, and, in 1909, was appointed second assistant light keeper at Devils Island Lighthouse, also in the Apostle Islands. By August 1910, he transferred to Split Rock for a promotion to assistant keeper for the new light station. He was just twenty-six.

At that time, Joseph had advanced to become the head light keeper at LaPointe Lighthouse near Ashland, Wisconsin—about forty miles away from Split Rock on Lake Superior's South Shore. Joseph heard rumors of Ed's drowning at Split Rock two days after the tragedy. In his official logbook for October 4, 1910, Joseph wrote about his duties and dreaded the worst: "Worked on the walk. Heard today that Ed Sexton was drowned. Hope not."

On October 5, 1910, Keeper Young was able to get a telegram to his superiors at the Lighthouse Service Eleventh District Headquarters in Detroit, informing them of the loss of the two keepers. Acting quickly by governmental standards, by late afternoon the same day an assistant keeper from the Duluth Range Light Station arrived at Split Rock to fill at least one of the vacancies left by the drowned keepers. The logbook for Split Rock shows that on October 6, 1910, Mrs. Sexton left for Duluth by way of a gasoline launch that came for her from Two Harbors. Keeper Young also reported that on October 12, William Gill arrived to look for his brother's body. Other entries to the log show that both Young and William Gill continued to search until Gill left Split Rock on October 23. The bodies were never found.

The official light station log reported many accidents and close calls over the years. One keeper contracted smallpox. Others fell off ladders. And an air compressor exploded next to a keeper. But the drowning deaths of assistant light keepers Edward Sexton and Roy G. Gill were the only fatalities ever associated with Split Rock in more than a half century of physical work on the cliff top.

Autumn sunrise, 2006

THERE IS NEVER a bad dawn over Lake Superior, but I think the most spectacular sunrises occur in October. For most of the spring and summer, the sun rises far enough north that if you stand along the shoreline in the state park west of the lighthouse and look toward the lighthouse, the sunrise is hidden from view behind the lighthouse cliff. Beginning at the summer solstice in late June, the sun begins to rise and set a little farther south every day. By mid-September, it appears right out of the lake when viewed from this shoreline spot. Each day the sun rises a few degrees farther out over the lake and farther away from the cliff and lighthouse. The autumn sun rises about two minutes later in the morning each day, around 7 AM in late September instead of around 5 AM as it does in June.

Since the lake has been warming up all summer, October mornings tend to be mild and comfortable. But, best of all, the autumn dawn skies display fantastic colors. Two factors contribute to the color storm: farm harvesting to the west, which raises more dust into the atmosphere, and smoke from wildfires in Canada and the western United States. Either way, the sky at sunrise is usually lit up with colors ranging from shades of orange and yellow to turquoise and lavender. On many autumn mornings, the lake grows calm, affording wonderful reflections of the sunrise colors. These mornings provided a perfect time to take a walk along the shoreline with my camera, or to just sit on the porch with a cup of coffee before starting a busy day.

Early on some autumn mornings, I tried to watch for the green flash at sunrise. I observed this meteorological optical phenomenon just a handful of times and was able to photograph it only once. The green flash, sometimes appearing as a green ray, lasts for a couple of seconds as the top edge of the sun appears over the horizon. It can also occur at sunset, as the top edge of the sun dips below the horizon. The light passes through the earth's atmosphere, which acts like a prism to cause the sun's light to separate into the colors of the spectrum. Atmospheric conditions must be just right for a distinct spot of green to appear for about two seconds. Other colors are refracted or absorbed. I have heard it is best observed over the oceans of the tropics, but it does happen on Lake Superior. If you are patient, you may be lucky enough to see it.

In late summer and early fall when air above the lake is at its warmest, it's a good time to watch for Lake Superior mirages. Called fata morgana, these mirages occur in the air above an object in the far distance when cool air is trapped beneath a warmer layer of air above. In calm weather,

A fata morgana is a type of mirage named for King Arthur's sister, a sorceress who was thought to use these traps to lure sailors into danger. This one appeared in June 2015.

PARK AND SITE, THE BEGINNINGS

The story of Split Rock Lighthouse State Park and the Split Rock Lighthouse Historic Site demonstrates what can happen when people work together to make a spectacular place available to many. It's a long story, and I'll tell a piece of it at a time.

Minnesota officials launched plans for a small state park around Split Rock Lighthouse as early as 1967, two years before the Coast Guard decommissioned Split Rock Light Station and shut off its beam. Several forward-looking state legislators realized the Coast Guard would soon walk away from Split Rock, leaving an abandoned lighthouse steeped in historic significance and valuable as a draw for tourism and recreation. The state already operated a nearby wayside stop on a small chunk of land that provided a great view of the lighthouse. The 1967 legislation designated it as Split Rock Lighthouse State Park, with authorization for expansion.

In the spring of 1969, the lighthouse and nearly eight acres of light station property were added to the National Register of Historic Places. Later that same year, Governor Harold LeVander decided the state should obtain the property and maintain it as a historic site. But the government can move slowly. The lighthouse grounds sat vacant from 1969 until early 1971. Grass grew long, paint peeled on the boarded-up buildings, but tourists continued to come—ignoring the signs, fences, and barriers that the Coast Guard had put up before it cleared out. The federal government slapped a reasonable price tag on the property, setting the acquisition value at $50,150. Luckily, the light station never hit the open market. Who knows what private ownership might have produced? Instead, the picturesque parcel was deeded to the State of Minnesota as "surplus property," with the requirement that it must be maintained as a historic site in perpetuity. The original smaller state park was expanded to include the lighthouse.

The DNR's precursor, known as the Minnesota Department of Conservation, breathed new life into slumbering Split Rock. In March 1971, the first state park manager, Frank Wotring, moved into the middle light keeper's dwelling. He became the next link in the chain, following Lighthouse Service and Coast Guard keepers.

The DNR leveled the ground for a new parking lot to embrace the onslaught of tourist traffic. But the state park was still tiny, with only a new access road from Highway 61 and a vault toilet next to the parking area. Through the 1970s and 1980s, DNR officials continued to acquire a patchwork of privately owned land between the lighthouse and the Split Rock River—adding further acquisitions inland from Highway 61. By 1977, the state park had expanded to nearly two thousand acres. It would take another decade, into the mid-1980s, to design and build the wonderful trails, popular picnic areas and campgrounds, the park road and buildings.

The DNR was living up to its primary mission at Split Rock: protecting the state's natural resources and providing recreation for growing numbers of visitors in those settings. DNR personnel stabilized the aging historic buildings, but preserving the historic light station was not their main priority.

Upper falls of Chapin's Creek, now known as Shipwreck Creek, May 2013

this layer of warmer air, called a temperature or thermal inversion, can act like a refracting lens and produce an inverted image. I have watched ore carriers sailing past the lighthouse, perhaps a dozen miles out on the lake, with a perfect image of the ship inverted directly above the real ship.

At other times, these layers of warmer air caused distant objects to appear much closer by compressing or stretching objects seen at long distances. The light is refracted downward and actually travels around the curvature of the earth. There were times when the South Shore of the lake near Cornucopia, Wisconsin—nearly thirty miles away—appeared so close that barns and fields were easily visible through binoculars. On one perfectly calm day in April, peering with binoculars through the dry, clear air over the lake, I saw the trees on the shoreline of the Keweenaw Peninsula on the Michigan South Shore. I found it hard to believe, so I confirmed the compass bearing and checked the official National Oceanic and Atmospheric Administration (NOAA) Lake Superior navigation chart that hangs in the visitor center. The peninsula is one hundred miles from Split Rock.

~

NEAR THE LIGHTHOUSE, a creek flowed out of the North Shore hills. In the 1920s, a fellow named Chapin built a large and comfortable cabin at its mouth, near a point commercial fishermen called Rust, Rusty, or Gold Point. The creek, known as Chapin's Creek among locals, was unimaginatively renamed Shipwreck Creek because it enters the lake near where the *Madeira* wrecked in 1905. It's not the only new name for these ancient places. Dakota, Cree, and Ojibwe people had names that are no longer known for places all over the North Shore.

The Chapin's Creek terrain in the hills behind Split Rock Lighthouse State Park became one of my favorite places along the North Shore. Straight inland from Lake Superior for about a mile and a half, the land

THOSE WHO CAME BEFORE

In the calm of an early morning sunrise when the fog rises from the lake like smoke or on an afternoon hike along the ridge above the lake, my mind would often turn to all the people who had passed this way before us. There is a long and rich story of those who made the North Shore their home.

People began living along the North Shore after the glaciers retreated from northern Minnesota, some ten thousand years ago—but the landscape was different. As the glacial ice sheets receded, the meltwater flooded the Lake Superior basin, forming Glacial Lake Duluth. The water level of the lake was hundreds of feet above its current level, and the lake drained at its western end, through what's now the St. Croix River. Old gravel beach ridges from several thousand years ago can still be found in several places along the higher ridges above the lake. The people who moved into this area lived in small groups and hunted big game, such as mastodons, giant beavers, moose, deer, and bear. It was a cooler and damper world. The power of the grinding ice sheets had scraped the exposed bedrock clean, and the vegetation that emerged would have looked more like the tundra of northern Canada. Partly because the waterline has changed so much

over time, little evidence has been found along the North Shore of these first Native Americans, known to archaeologists as "Paleo-Indians"—and to many Native Americans as ancestors.

Around 3000 BCE, and for the following two millennia, people in this area made tools of copper. They found exposed outcrops of native copper along the South Shore of Lake Superior, as well as on Isle Royale, twenty miles off the North Shore. The metal was so pure that it could be hammered into tools and spear points. Shallow pits now mark where they mined it. In the late 1800s, a copper spearpoint was found on the small island near East Beaver Bay, about five miles up the shore from the lighthouse. This shows that native people were living along the North Shore as many as five thousand years ago.

By the early 1600s, Dakota and Cree people were living in what is now northern Minnesota; Ojibwe people (also known as Anishinaabe or Chippewa), who had moved over centuries from their homelands in the east, were living on the South Shore. For many years, the Ojibwe were the intermediaries of the fur trade, exchanging furs for goods with the French and goods for furs with the Dakota. By the late 1600s, rises in rocky knobs and outcrops to the highest ridge. It is rolling, rugged country covered with birch, balsam fir, and alder and a few remnant old pines from before the logging days. Land managers technically call these higher ridges the Superior Uplands. Back in the early 1980s, there were few trails besides those for snowmobiles that crisscrossed through the forest. In a few places, the old railroad grades are still visible. They were built by the Split Rock Lumber Company and used to log the area from 1896 to 1903.

~~~

the French had reached the western end of the lake, and by the 1780s they had built fur posts at Grand Portage and Fond du Lac (on the St. Louis River near Duluth). But when French traders upset the alliances among the tribes, the cooperation between the Dakota and Ojibwe ended, and warfare ensued. The Ojibwe moved onto the North Shore, the Dakota moved west and south, and the French continued a bustling fur trade with the Ojibwe and the Cree. French Canadian voyageurs paddled thirty-six-foot-long, Montreal birch-bark canoes loaded with ninety-pound packs of trade goods and topped with beaver pelts beneath the cliff where the lighthouse stands.

For all these centuries, people traveled in birchbark canoes up and down the North Shore, and Little Two Harbors would have been a convenient stopping point. Places where stone tools were manufactured and campsites from these years have been found in Split Rock Lighthouse State Park near the shore, but not at the top of the outcrop.

In 1854, the US government forced the Ojibwe to sign the Treaty of La Pointe and move to reservations, including Fond du Lac and Grand Portage. This opened northeastern Minnesota to settlement—and mining and logging. Prospectors flooded in, looking for copper, iron, silver, and gold. They were quickly followed by the lumber companies. From 1896 to 1903 the Split Rock Lumber Company ran a camp of nearly three hundred men at the mouth of the Split Rock River, and they laid ten miles of logging railroad track into the forest around the river—the area that is now Split Rock Lighthouse State Park. By 1910, the logging companies had stripped the North Shore of its old-growth pine forests.

European immigrants, mostly Scandinavian and German, also moved to the North Shore. In 1854, German immigrants founded Beaver Bay at the mouth of the Beaver River. Norwegian immigrants may have found Lake Superior and the rugged North Shore to be reminders of the fjords and inlets at home. Many became commercial fishermen, first for the lake trout and later for the abundant herring. By 1900, nearly every cove from Two Harbors to Grand Portage held a dock, a boathouse, and the home of a fisherman. Evidence of these fishing shanties can be seen at Little Two Harbors and in every cove in the state park.

ON CRISP FALL DAYS, especially after the kids were older, I loved to get away for a few hours. I grabbed my 20-gauge shotgun, threw a few shotgun shells in an old hunting vest, and put a bell on Shamus, our yellow Lab. We hiked down the park entrance road, crossed the highway, and disappeared into the hills to the north. Shamus and I ostensibly hunted the elusive ruffed grouse, but mainly we just rambled the rock domes and outcrops and creek bottoms.

A remnant white pine stump, October 2018

When we ranged north of Highway 61, most of the signs of human activity we came across were from the logging era. A few old railroad grades
date back to the turn of the twentieth century—left behind by the Split
Rock Lumber Company. From 1896 to 1903, it ran a lumber camp at the
mouth of the Split Rock River and built about ten miles of small-gauge
railroad spur line that fanned out from the river valley. As many as 250
men worked these woods for the company, sawing and dropping by hand

Logs in the boom on Split Rock
River, about 1907. *MNHS*

the stately old-growth white pines that blanketed the North Shore. They
loaded the logs onto railroad cars and dumped them into the dammed-up
mouth of the Split Rock River. Today you can still see huge posts from
that coffer dam, driven into the river bottom where the river flows into the
lake. When the dam opened, tugboats pulled huge rafts of pine logs across
Lake Superior to mills on the South Shore.

The hundred-year-old evidence of this logging activity remains visible
in the white pine stumps still standing back in the woods. The old-growth
pines had grown slowly for hundreds of years when the lumbermen felled
them. The wood was thick with resin, which is resistant to weathering.
Walking through the second-growth forest that exists today, I found these

old stumps surviving best on the dry, well-drained, south-facing slopes. The massive size of these old trees can be imagined, thanks to the large weathered stumps that remain—many of them four feet across. The loss of this ancient forest is regrettable, and every time I walk through the scrubby second growth that replaced it, I can only imagine the majesty of that forest. Remnants of the old-growth pines can still be seen between the two tunnels along Highway 61 in a tract of land owned and preserved by the Encampment Forest Association.

The witness post above Split Rock Lighthouse, January 2018

As I walked through the woods, I noticed that many of these stumps were charred. After the logging operation had cut the trees and harvested the logs, they left the slash from their cuttings everywhere. When they felled a tree, they cut off all its limbs and left them on the forest floor. Within a few years this debris grew bone dry. In 1908, wildfires burned up and down the North Shore. I discovered a so-called witness post at a section corner on a hilltop above Chapin's Creek behind the state park, still standing where surveyors planted it when this area was first charted in 1906. When the section lines were established, the surveyors walked each line that designated the mile-square sections. If the corner of four sections met on a prominent hilltop, they carved a square post out of a nearby white cedar tree and inscribed the section numbers on the four sides of the post and drove it in the ground. Those carved numbers were easy to read when I first found the witness post in the 1980s. Every few years, I returned to visit the post. After thirty-five years, the post had weathered considerably. Each time I visited, I piled a few rocks around the base to make sure it stayed in place. I hope it's still there.

I found a detailed reference to the 1908 fires while researching Ralph Russell Tinkham, the US Lighthouse Service engineer who oversaw the building of Split Rock Light Station in 1909. In September 1908,

Tinkham sailed as a passenger aboard the steamer *America,* heading up
the North Shore from Duluth to Grand Marais. He kept a daily journal,
and on September 13, 1908, he wrote,

> There were no fires that I noticed amounting to anything
> until we arrived off Split Rock. Here they said they were
> fighting fires down to within a half mile of the settlement
> [the logging camp at the mouth of Split Rock River]. Corun-
> dum Pt. and the next Pt. above that—the one Split Rock Lt.
> Sta. is to be erected upon—were all burned over as well as
> the mainland back of them, and still burning. ... There are
> 40 firefighters under firemen from Duluth to be landed on
> the north shore to fight the fires. ... At Grand Marais they
> landed to work south. ... The fire was close to the town and
> they were fighting night and day. The Naval Reserve boat,
> Gopher of Duluth was there for relief.

Many of these ancient white pine stumps left in the woods back of
Split Rock Lighthouse State Park are preserved by the carbon in the char-
ring from the slash fires of the logging era.

Today even the second-growth birch, the trees that grew up after the
pine were logged, are mostly dying and gone. That leaves a mosaic of balsam fir, alder brush, and spruce growing up in the forest succession that
has played out on the North Shore and elsewhere in northern Minnesota.

On one hike up Chapin's Creek with Shamus, I saw only about a half
dozen of the old-growth white pine giants that escaped the saws and
axes a century ago. When we reached the top of Christmas Tree Ridge,
it heartened me to see many small pines growing up there. They looked
young, but they were probably overlooked a hundred years ago, considered too hard to reach. They are dwarfed as a result of growing on the
thin soil of rocky ridges. There was something soothing about walking
among these survivors, crossing the bed of orange pine needles that blanketed the forest floor. All was silence until the passing ravens shared their
thoughts with one another.

From a point of rocks over the treetops, I could just make out the top
of the lighthouse almost two miles away and some five hundred feet below us. The wind gently blew up the hill from the lake and road, bringing
the murmur of traffic on Highway 61. The Superior Hiking Trail follows

the high point of the ridgeline, and we took the trail through old-growth white pines for a mile or so. The dog flushed a couple of grouse that I didn't have a shot at, or didn't care to try. Standing on the ridgetop, watching the sun nearing the horizon to the southwest, we felt a chill rising up from the forest below. So we headed for home, a short hour-long walk in the gathering dusk. It was comforting, and not at all frightening, to know that there was no one else within two miles of me amid the thick woods. I knew where home was and how to get there. The dog trusted me, and I

Shamus on Christmas Tree Ridge, February 2017. The lighthouse is in the distance, a tiny spike above his head.

trusted him. This was home. I loved this place more than any other. But I couldn't wait to get back to our keeper's house. We headed downhill, back toward the lake, where lights and family welcomed us near the lighthouse. It was so warm and comfortable to be with Jane and the kids again. I could leave a part of me back on the ridgetop with no contradictions. A part of me was always there, on the ridge—just like a part of me was always back home at the lighthouse.

〜〜

ALONG THE NORTH SHORE, the door quickly slams shut on autumn, and winter takes hold with the coming of the big storms that barrel across Lake Superior out of the northeast—the infamous "gales of November." Between late October and early December, weather patterns change as frigid northern winds push down out of Canada over the waters of Lake Superior that have been slowly warming all summer. While we grew saddened to see fall come to an end, Jane and I loved the power of these storms. To stand in the teeth of a nor'easter was to feel, see, and hear incredible forces at work. As the skies darken to a consistent slate gray, winds pick up out of the northeast. Depending on the power and the size of the low-pressure weather system, these winds blow up to fifty or even sixty miles per hour—sometimes roaring for a few hours, other times for a few days. With nothing to slow down the system over hundreds of miles of open lake, the wind can build monstrous waves more than twenty feet high.

Behind these storms follow the first of the cold fronts out of Canada, Alaska, and Siberia. The winds die down. The skies clear to an incredible blue. And the temperatures plummet. While it takes months before the big lake begins to freeze, all the rest of the world around is locked in ice—ready for the snows of winter.

2.
≋ *Winter* ≋

The change to winter comes slowly, in fits and starts. The days are shorter, the shadows longer. Temperatures drop with each new storm. By now, my winter preparations were nearly complete. Storm windows were up. Firewood was split and stacked. Shovels, snowblowers, and snowshoes were ready, and the pantry was stocked. To prevent the pipes from freezing, I wrapped heat tape on the water pipe from the well head, located six feet outside the house. I staked frost blankets—usually used to overwinter perennial plants—to the ground over the sewer lines snaking to the septic mounds. These kept frost from penetrating the ground to the depth of the buried pipes. We set mouse traps in all the critical locations in the houses.

The early winter days of November and December became the toughest to endure. This is the time of year when night arrives in the late afternoon and the sun waits to emerge until after breakfast. From my living room perch, I watched the dusk set in. I knew by heart exactly where the sun would set to the southwest on the winter solstice. At a few minutes after four in the afternoon on the shortest day of the year, it disappeared behind the shoulder of Day Hill—a prominent flat-topped basalt dome in the state park about a mile away. From late December on, I watched with great anticipation for spring. The sun set just a tiny bit farther north each afternoon.

≈≈

MOST WINTER DAYS, the sky was a solid leaden gray with low, thick clouds blurring the horizon. The light station is built on a point, so when you gaze from northeast to southwest from Split Rock, Lake Superior meets that horizon. The big lake can make its own weather. Some days, the sky over the lake is fair, while it is overcast and dark over the North Shore. On those days, the sun sparkles off the bright *continued on page 47*

THE WORKINGS OF THE LIGHT

An exquisite technological marvel, the classical Fresnel lighthouse lens at Split Rock has a French pedigree. Pronounced "fray-NEL," the lens arranges prisms to reflect, refract, and magnify light into a narrow beam. French scientist Augustin-Jean Fresnel patented the navigational breakthrough in 1821. But it took thirty years before the United States started buying the superior French lenses to replace its woefully inadequate lighthouse lenses and reflectors.

Lucky for us, when the US Coast Guard decommissioned Split Rock Light Station in 1969, it left the lens in the lighthouse. We are equally fortunate that the State of Minnesota was willing to step in and preserve the lighthouse and all its mechanical wonders. At nearly every lighthouse that the Coast Guard "disestablished"—to use government parlance—workers quickly removed the lens and all the working mechanisms. They feared vandals. The Coast Guard puts an insurance value of $750,000 on assemblies such as the one at Split Rock.

Our lighthouse on Lake Superior is an outlier in more than a geographic way. The Coast Guard typically retained ownership and responsibility for the lenses, even when it transferred decommissioned lighthouses to museums or governmental agencies. At Split Rock, the State of Minnesota enjoys full ownership of the lens and the lighthouse, with the Minnesota Historical Society overseeing its preservation.

Each classical Fresnel lens assembly features four main components: the lens with its prisms; a lamp to provide the light source; a system to rotate the lens, either chariot wheels or, beginning in the 1890s, a mercury float upon which the lens revolves; and a clockwork mechanism with its weights and pulleys. Each part has a story.

— THE LENS

Split Rock's Fresnel lens is called a *bivalve* or *clamshell lens* because it's really two identical lenses placed back-to-back. It's the second largest on the Great Lakes, and its beam is visible at least twenty-two miles away. Split Rock's lens is seven feet wide, contains 252 prism panels, and rotates once every twenty seconds—emitting a flash out on the lake every ten seconds, given its two halves rotating opposite each other. The lens is perched on a cast-iron platform and pedestal attached to the mercury bearing and clockwork. The whole thing weighs more than three tons.

LEFT: Fresnel lens, 1990. *Jet Lowe, Historic American Engineering Record, Library of Congress*
ABOVE: Interior of the lantern, 1990. *Jet Lowe, Historic American Engineering Record, Library of Congress*

— THE LAMP

The original source of the beacon's light was an incandescent oil-vapor lamp, fueled by kerosene. It was somewhat like a Coleman camping lantern, only much more sophisticated; it burned an average of one gallon of kerosene each night, and up to two gallons on the long nights of early winter. This fuel, delivered in tanks by the lighthouse tender boats, was stored in the oil house a short distance from the lighthouse. Each evening the keeper filled a brass can with kerosene, carried it up the spiral staircase to the lamp, and filled a reservoir tank that was mounted to the pedestal of the lens and connected to the lamp through a vaporizer tube. He pumped the tank to put the kerosene under pressure, then lit an alcohol torch to warm the vaporizer tube for eight to ten minutes and start the lamp. The mantle of the kerosene lamp provided a brilliant white light comparable to the thousand-watt light bulb that replaced it in 1940 when the light station was electrified.

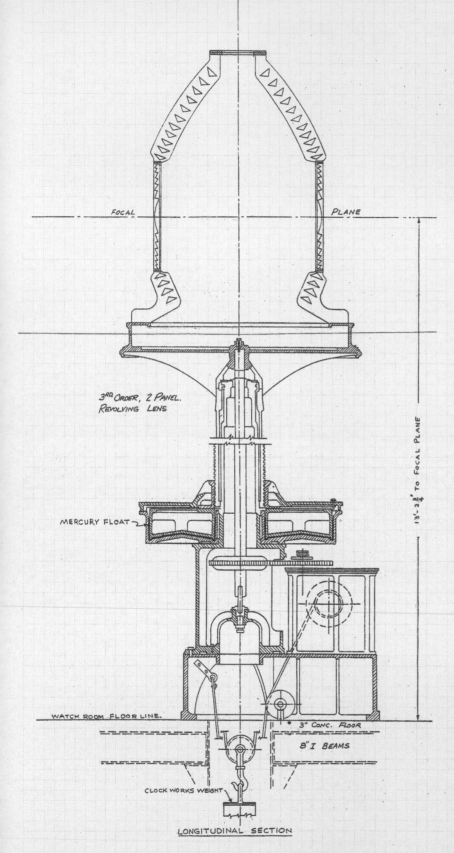

FOCAL   PLANE

3ʳᴰ ORDER, 2 PANEL.
REVOLVING LENS

13'-2¾' TO FOCAL PLANE

MERCURY FLOAT

WATCH ROOM FLOOR LINE.

3" CONC. FLOOR

8" I BEAMS

CLOCK WORKS WEIGHT

LONGITUDINAL SECTION

The lens assembly, as drawn on linen by the US Lighthouse Service, 1908. *National Archives*

— THE MERCURY BEARING

Many Split Rock visitors wonder how a 1,500-pound lens spins so quietly and effortlessly. Six quarts of mercury do the trick, housed in a cast-iron bowl at the lens's base. A cast-iron float fits snugly inside that bowl of mercury. Imagine two Bundt pans, with one floating on the mercury inside the other. Mercury is so dense that the lens literally floats on a thin half-inch layer.

Fresnel lenses have rotated on mercury bearings since the 1890s. Before that, bronze wheels rotated the lens. The advent of mercury complicated lighthouse operations, because the dense element evaporates slowly and its fumes can be toxic to humans. But light keepers avoided exposure to mercury vapor at dangerous levels. It simply wasn't their job to handle the mercury. If major work were required on the lens assembly, a specially trained "lampist" would be called in.

Dust, dead flies, and other debris in the mercury slowed lens revolutions at times, so—very infrequently—draining and cleaning the mercury and the bowl was required. I performed this task twice, with trepidation, in 1983 and 2009. The first time, with the help of our maintenance man, Pete Melnotte, I researched the old float systems and the hazards of mercury vapor. We chose a cool November day after the site closed for the season. Mercury is more stable and emits less vapor in cooler temperatures. We opened all the windows in the lighthouse before we unsealed and removed the cast-iron covers from the float bowl. We then opened the spigot on the bottom of the

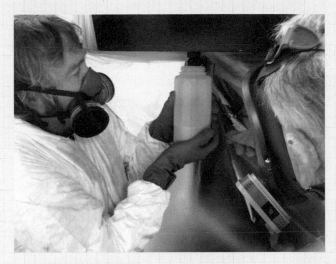

Draining the mercury, 2009

The mercury float, raised, showing mercury in the bowl, 2009

bowl and slowly drained the mercury into solid pails. Liquid mercury is 13.5 times heavier than water, so if you fill a gallon milk jug with mercury it would weigh 112 pounds. We then skimmed off the dead flies, spiders, dust, and rust scale that had accumulated in the cast-iron bowl. Mercury is so thick that a silver dollar will float on its surface. All the gunk sat atop the mercury, so it was easy to skim off—like schmaltz floating atop chicken soup. We wore respirators and mercury-monitoring badges to warn us if exposure reached dangerous levels. After securing the spigot, we poured the cleaned mercury back into the large cast-iron bowl. It was fascinating to watch the mercury lift the three-quarter-ton lens, allowing it to float and spin.

Our 2009 lens project was far more involved. We drained the six quarts of liquid mercury from the float bowl, then cleaned the bowl and the mercury before replacing it. The Minnesota Department of Health monitored the work because of health hazards from mercury exposure. Five of us suited up in full hazardous-material suits with respirators. Jim Woodward and Kurt Fosburg, a pair of Coast Guard–qualified lampists, first removed the cast-iron covers over the float bowl. Then they raised the float out of

the bowl by rotating it up the large threads on the lens pedestal. For the first time in fifty years, the interior of the mercury bowl was fully exposed.

Carl Herbrandson from the Minnesota Department of Health and Ed Swain from the Minnesota Pollution Control Agency monitored the levels of mercury vapors in the air with a Lumex machine. It looks like a portable vacuum cleaner, only with sophisticated sensors. Exposure readings on Carl's laptop spiked as soon as the bowl was opened. It took the lampists a few hours to drain the mercury, clean the bowl, refill it with the six quarts of mercury, and lower the large float back down to rest on the mercury. I took photographs and shot video of the entire procedure, peppering them with questions about the lens assembly. Before they sealed up the bowl, I asked them to pour one quart of pure mineral oil on top of the mercury. This sealed the mercury from exposure to the air in the lens room. We watched the graph measuring mercury exposure drop quickly to safe levels. After inspecting all the gears and bearings and lubricating the moving parts, the lampists confirmed that the century-old Split Rock lens assembly was in surprisingly excellent condition. What a huge relief.

The gears that drive the mechanism, 1990. *Jet Lowe, Historic American Engineering Record, Library of Congress*

— THE CLOCKWORK MECHANISM

Like a grandfather clock, the bearings and gears of the lens's clock mechanism keep precise time—assuring the lens rotates to flash its beacon every ten seconds. This clockwork requires rewinding every two hours before the weights reach the bottom of the lighthouse, twenty-five feet below. If the weights hit bottom, the lens stops turning. In Split Rock's active era, keepers climbed to the top of the tower, inserted the crank handle in the clockwork mechanism, and cranked 150 times to wind the weights back to the top—every two hours, all night long.

Their burden eased in 1940, when the Coast Guard wired the light station for electricity and installed an electric motor to rotate the lens. No more climbing the tower and winding up the weights every two hours. The Coast Guard also replaced the kerosene oil-vapor lamp with an electric lamp changer that burned a thousand-watt incandescent light bulb. From then on, keepers simply flipped one switch to turn on the lamp and one switch to prompt the motor to rotate the lens. They flipped the switch on a half hour before sunset and flipped it off a half hour after sunrise. They also installed a warning alarm from the lighthouse to each keeper's dwelling that would notify them if the power went out or the light quit revolving. At last, keepers could sleep through the night uninterrupted. Gone were the four-hour night shifts for each man.

In my book, the lens assembly is the true star of the show at Split Rock. For the early keepers, it proved to be the pivotal part of their job. For me, it also felt like a huge responsibility. Not only is the lens assembly beautiful and costly, it's irreplaceable.

We assessed the light assembly four times during my thirty-six years managing the site. Once, experts stabilized and sealed the red-and-white lead putty that holds the prisms in place in their brass frame. Over time, this putty dries out and becomes crumbly, putting the prisms at risk of falling from the lens frame. The specialists used a hypodermic needle to inject a liquid resin called B-72 into the putty to harden it.

Preserving the Split Rock lens assembly was my longtime goal. I wanted to keep the mechanisms in good working condition in their original locations so we could show lighthouse visitors how the light was designed to operate. A lighthouse without a lens and a beacon is just a shell of what it once was. To see the beacon sweeping out across the lake brings the lighthouse to life—enhancing our appreciation of the light keepers and their critical role guiding the ships.

blue water like a billion diamonds. But that sun never climbs too high over the southern horizon—even at midday. The small, dark silhouette of a Great Lakes freighter might pass by, some fifteen miles out on the lake. Lit from behind by the low sun, gigantic ore carriers called lakers stand out in contrast to the bright lake. Lakers load taconite at the North Shore ports of Silver Bay, Two Harbors, and Duluth-Superior, then travel east to the lake outlet at Sault Ste. Marie. (Sault, pronounced "soo," is French for rapids, and the Soo Locks were built to move ships around them.) They deliver as much tonnage as possible to the smelters down on Lake Erie before mid-January, when the Soo Locks close for the season.

Lake Superior dominated both my family's life and our views, as it surrounded us on three sides. The big lake's presence seemed most notable during the winter months. I watched with fascination as the lake responded daily to the growing winds and falling temperatures. The surface temperature of Lake Superior warms all summer long and, because it's such a vast body of water, it takes longer than the small inland lakes to

Winter solstice sunset, 2008

cool as winter approaches. These warmer water temperatures at the lake surface help keep the shores around the lake warmer than the higher elevations rising away from the lake. It often snows just a mile or two inland in November and December, while along the shore we face a messy mix of rain and snow.

November marks a huge transition in northland weather patterns. The warm, humid air coming up from the Gulf of Mexico gives way to polar winds howling down from the Canadian Arctic. These two systems often clash over Lake Superior. Massive low-pressure systems swirl out of the northeast, barreling down on Split Rock from across the lake. These storms often grow into sloppy two-day affairs, with rain and snow blowing sideways before gale-force winds. These are the infamous "gales of November" that wrecked so many ships over the years—including the *Edmund Fitzgerald*.

~~~

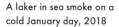

A laker in sea smoke on a cold January day, 2018

OVER THE YEARS, we hunkered down in our house near the lighthouse through many nor'easters. These storms packed sleet, snow, and powerful winds right off the lake. We clocked northeast winds at seventy-seven miles per hour during the worst of these blows. The winds usually blew all day and night, whipping up twenty-foot-high waves that swelled across nearly 250 miles of open water between the Canadian shore to the northeast and Split Rock. Many times the wind ripped a storm window right off one of the houses.

PURLOINED ARTIFACTS

We learned a lesson that first winter. On a foggy and gray Sunday afternoon early in December 1982—a mere month after I started my job as the resident historic site manager—I was painting walls in our new home in the middle keeper's dwelling. Traffic on Highway 61 was typically light in December, with few visitors. The leaves were gone, deer hunting was over, and it was too early for skiing and snowmobiling. Nice and quiet.

Jane was out in the yard when two young guys, dressed a little rough, and a timid-looking woman stopped to look at the lighthouse. The two men asked questions that quickly set off some alarms for Jane. She came in and told me they were asking if people live in all of the houses and what they stored. I put down my paintbrush, shrugged into a jacket, and headed outside for a casual chat. After asking a few questions about the lighthouse, they started grilling me about the restored keeper's dwelling. *How old were the furnishings? How valuable? Were we the only ones living at the lighthouse?*

Something didn't smell right about this trio, so I started to ask some friendly questions. "Are you just playing tourist and seeing the sites?"

They replied, "No, we're headed to Lutsen to try to get jobs at the ski hill."

I followed up: "Are you staying in the area?"

"Yeah, we're staying in Beaver Bay tonight."

Short of following them to the parking lot to

"HE'S CLIMBING OUT THE BATHROOM WINDOW—AND HE'S GOT A KNIFE!"

record the make of their car and write down their license plate, that was about all I could do. I wished them well as they went on their way.

The next morning, after kissing Jane goodbye, I headed out for the thirty-second walk to my office in the third keeper's dwelling, next door. It had once provided housing for the second assistant keeper. It was the farthest from the lighthouse, among the three identical houses. As soon as I unlocked the door I could feel the cold air, and I found a broken window in the living room, which doubled as my office. A quick inspection revealed missing items from the collection of artifacts that had been stored in the house for the winter. The site's petty cash was also gone from my desk.

I immediately called the Lake County Sheriff's Office to say that there had been a burglary overnight at Split Rock. They dispatched a deputy. Thinking about my conversation with the scruffy visitors from the previous afternoon, I quickly called the Beaver Bay Motel—the closest lodging place to Split Rock at the time and the only one in Beaver Bay. After several agonizing rings, the front desk clerk answered and confirmed that two men and a woman staying there matched my description. They were still at the motel, but she thought that they were packing to leave.

Just then, two county deputies arrived in a police cruiser, and they questioned me at length about the burglary and my suspicions about the travelers. I told them about the trio's plans to stay in Beaver Bay, my call to the front desk at the motel, and the suspects' plans to hit the road any minute. In my mind, the deputies were way too lackadaisical. I was impatient for them to get after the suspects. I tried to convince them that, if we hurried, we could catch them at the motel. But the deputies kept poking around my office, dusting for fingerprints, and looking for tire tracks in the parking lot. They finally sauntered out to their cruiser. As an afterthought, they asked Jane and me to come along to identify the three. Much to my disappointment, they decided that neither lights nor sirens were needed for the five-mile drive from Split Rock to Beaver Bay. That drive seemed to take forever.

In the company of two of Lake County's finest deputies, we rolled up to the stodgy old Beaver Bay Motel. As we pulled up in the police cruiser, I recognized one of the suspected burglars hauling a familiar box to the motel's dumpster, and I told the deputies that it was the kind we used to store artifacts. Spying the sheriff's vehicle, the alleged crook quickly skulked back to his room, where we observed a second face peering out through the window.

"Nailed 'em," I said as we got out of the cruiser.

Jane and I kept our distance. The deputies received permission to look around the room, and that was when I heard one of them shout, "There's another one, and he's climbing out the bathroom window—and he's got a knife!"

The deputies pulled the guy back in through the window and wrested the knife from him. All three were subdued, and we recovered a few artifacts that had been thrown out the bathroom window on the backside of the motel. The desperadoes were cuffed and hauled off to the Silver Bay City Jail. Jane and I sure wondered later about the way it went down. The officers asked Jane and me to come into the motel room during the arrest. Since one of the suspects was a female, they wanted Jane to be present. It didn't feel like the safest of circumstances.

A few days later, one of the deputies called to ask us to come to the Silver Bay jail to sit in on the questioning of the two male suspects. The small table in the holding area was barely big enough for us and the two deputies, who questioned the accused one at a time. The jail was so small that, as the deputies questioned one of the men, the other one could listen from his cell—shouting all sorts of accusations about his buddy ratting him out. We recovered all of the artifacts—nothing of great value, worth little to them—but not the petty cash. My reward was in just catching these miscreants.

I later learned from the sheriff's office that all three of these characters had lengthy records and that the two men ended up serving sentences for their Split Rock misadventure. After this brush with crime, I upped my morning and evening patrols of the historic site, and Jane and I realized the importance of security at Split Rock.

Waves driven by a nor'easter slam the coast below the lighthouse, hidden in trees, 2018. The sound is deafening.

The pounding of these waves against the cliff rattled the windows in our house. The spray shot straight up the face to the top of the 130-foot Split Rock cliff—lashing sideways in the wind. When temperatures dropped, this spray froze on everything it hit. After some of these storms, an inches-thick ice glaze coated trees, rocks, chain-link fences, parking lots, sidewalks, and all the light station buildings. The ice casing hardened on trees and power lines—but what a sight when the sun came out and transformed the world into a glittering, dazzling ice kingdom.

Countering the beauty, power outages came with these storms. With no electrical power, the furnace went out. With no heat for any length of time, we worried about the water freezing in radiators and pipes in the house. A freeze in the cast-iron radiators would split them open like coconuts. No electricity meant no well pump and no water from the well. It also knocked out the sump pump in the basement, which moved water from sinks and toilets out of the house to the septic mounds. The other two keepers' dwellings and the visitor center were also at risk. Luckily, these storms were so massive that the US Weather Service could forecast them days in advance, so we had plenty of time to prepare. We hauled the

portable camping toilet into the house from the storage barn and the kids filled the bathtub so we had a supply of fresh water on hand. We broke out lanterns and flashlights from the basement. As the wind and waves intensified, the old, leaky windows rattled and the curtains swayed in time with the gusts. I lit a small fire in the backup woodstove in the basement to ease the chill. We crossed our fingers, hoping that falling trees would miss the lines supplying power to the lighthouse. In the early years, if a line did go down, we might be without power for up to three days. Later, the power company got better, and it would seldom be out for more than several hours.

Real cold set in when winter grew serious. Every year around New Year's Day, we braced for one of the coldest weeks of the year. Weather forecasters adopted the term "polar vortex" to describe the conditions that drop down from Canada and settle over northern Minnesota and Lake Superior. The sky clears to a crisp, bright blue, and the thermometer fails to top zero for a few days. Water vapor rises off the open lake in gigantic billowing clouds. Old commercial fishermen called it sea smoke or frost smoke. And the frigid northwest wind sends it skimming low across the lake to the South Shore.

This dark and sloppy time of year was unpopular among North Shore visitors. At Split Rock, we could catch our breath after the high tourist traffic during summer and fall. I could plan for the coming summer season, still some five months away. Winter was the time to switch gears: work with my program manager to start planning programs for the upcoming year, prepare the site's annual budget, write and conduct staff performance reviews, plan equipment repairs and purchases with my maintenance man, plow snow, write interpretive manuals, plow snow some more, develop a site marketing plan, meet with donors or legislators, plow snow again, work with the museum store manager on merchandise orders, schedule school groups for summer tours, and finally, as spring approached, advertise for, interview, hire, and train new staff for the upcoming season. But a slower flow of tourists didn't mean that no one headed up Highway 61 to visit Split Rock Lighthouse. In fact, traffic remained high enough that in the early 2000s we started keeping the visitor center open five days a week. We closed only on Tuesdays and Wednesdays, when traffic was lowest. We didn't charge a fee, as none of

OPPOSITE: Inspecting a mountain ash encased in ice by a storm's waves, 1985

The lake steams with sea smoke over open water at minus 35 degrees Fahrenheit, February 2, 1996.

the historic buildings were open, but people could walk the grounds. Winter weekends were always busy, with up to a couple hundred people visiting the site. Mondays, Thursdays, and Fridays were a little quieter. That left Tuesdays and Wednesdays for us to clean and repair the visitor center as necessary, and to hold staff meetings uninterrupted. I credit the advent of digital photography and social media, along with enhanced winter clothing, for turning everyone into a photographer willing to brave wintry conditions in hopes of capturing memorable images of the lighthouse and the lake.

~~~

THE QUIETER DAYS of early winter meant I had more time to spend with my family at our lighthouse home. The nights fully darkened by 5 PM, and the sun wouldn't come up for some fifteen hours. This far north, there were barely eight hours of sunlight at the end of December. Once

PARK AND SITE, CREATING SPACES FOR VISITORS

Much of my work in the winter involved finding ways to improve the visitors' experiences. This work had been evolving for years at Split Rock, as the site was separated from the park.

In 1976, the setup at Split Rock had changed in response to a new law known as the Minnesota Outdoor Recreation Act. This legislation gave the Minnesota Historical Society, which had demonstrated its ability to preserve and interpret historic sites, responsibility for several Minnesota cultural and historic sites that sat within state parks: Split Rock Lighthouse, Historic Forestville, Fort Ridgely, and the Lindbergh House in Little Falls. All told, twenty-five acres at Split Rock were transferred to the society, including the original seven-plus acres of the light station. Tom Ellig became the society's first historic site manager at Split Rock and moved into the middle keeper's dwelling with his young family. By 1978, the two DNR families that lived in light keeper dwellings moved out.

This was the start of a dynamic partnership. The Minnesota Historical Society introduced programs at the historic site, while the DNR managed the state park surrounding the light station. Blending two large branches of state government can be tricky. Some DNR personnel shifted to offices at Gooseberry Falls State Park, seven miles southwest down the shoreline. In those years, finances were not an issue, as the state legislature funded the historical society staff at the lighthouse and the costs of historic restoration and interpretation. The DNR, meanwhile, continued to collect fees for state park permits that visitors to the lighthouse were required to purchase.

By 1982, Tom Ellig resigned after six years as the first historic site manager at Split Rock to take over supervision of historic sites in southern Minnesota. I was thrilled and honored when the society hired me to take the job. Tom had laid the groundwork for much of what was coming. Between 1976 and 1982, he and the society's managers drew up a master plan for the development of the site and worked on initial ideas for a visitor center. Tom also oversaw work to restore the head light keeper's dwelling, as well as the Fresnel lens and its mechanism in the lighthouse. For that project, he recruited Tom Gould, a Two Harbors jeweler and watch repairer, to disassemble and clean the giant clockwork mechanism that revolves the 1,500-pound lens.

I was lucky, arriving in 1982 and riding the momentum that had built at Split Rock in the 1970s. It may sound obvious to say it, but trouble can arise when two separate state agencies—the DNR and the Minnesota Historical Society—simultaneously develop plans and seek funding. In this case, though, we worked together and cooperated, setting the stage for new and exciting developments for the growing number of visitors to Split Rock.

Jane and I experienced those changes directly. We had grown accustomed to packing a lunch and hiking with our golden retriever, Ozzie, through the remote and undeveloped woods, creeks, ravines, and rock outcrops between Lake Superior and Highway 61—from the lighthouse all the way to the Split Rock River. The only public access to this area was the scenic overlook right next to the Split Rock Trading Post on Highway 61. About a half mile down the highway from the overlook, a rough trail snaked from a small parking lot on the highway to the top of Day Hill. There was also a wayside rest parking lot at the mouth of the Split Rock River.

The visitor center was expanded in 2003.

All that changed in 1984 when the DNR began building a new park road from the entrance to the lighthouse deep down into the state park. This mile-long road paralleled the lakeshore between the lake and Highway 61. Twenty campsites soon sprung up at the end of the road for cart-in camping. The campground was a perfect fit for this state park, with sites spaced at a respectable distance from each other along the shore or back in the birch forest. When the campground opened in 1985, it was designed for tent campers only. That kept the visitors' impact low. New picnic sites were soon added near the shore, along with a trail center building connected by the hiking trail about a third of a mile down from the lighthouse. Trails from the lighthouse, past Day Hill and Corundum Point all the way to the Split Rock River, opened and provided scenic routes for hiking in the summer and cross-country skiing in the winter. In those hectic days in the mid-1980s, the DNR also built a new and bigger park office, as well as a maintenance building in the old right-of-way of the original road to the lighthouse that the Civilian Conservation Corps first laid down in 1935.

While the DNR expanded the state park into a coveted destination for North Shore visitors, the Minnesota Historical Society was busy upgrading facilities at the historic site. These were heady times for me as the site manager. The legislature approved funding in 1984 for construction of a visitor center, as well as restoring and stabilizing the seventy-five-year-old light station buildings. My job was to help plan a building that would meet the needs of the growing number of visitors. I was to visualize the best facility for tours and interpretive programs and then share that information with the historical society's curators and interpretive staff, who would flesh out a professional program. The challenges included planning an exhibit hall and an interpretive film for the auditorium, as well as expanding tours. The historical society hired an architect and a construction contractor. I gained an amazing amount of knowledge working with them.

When the new center opened in July 1986, it was quite an upgrade. Up until then, our center of operations was the third keeper's dwelling, farthest from the lighthouse. The kitchen was our break room, and my office was in the parlor; interpreters changed into costumes in the bedrooms upstairs. What a luxury for us all to move to the visitor center, where there was plenty of space and privacy. I enjoyed having a real office. Computers, internet, and wi-fi were still several years away. In the meantime, I communicated with my boss by long-distance phone call or snail mail. But best of all, visitors could enjoy a modern building with exhibits and a theater, a well-stocked gift shop, and fully accessible restrooms.

supper was done and the kids completed their homework, we often played cards or a board game. Television was hit or miss at Split Rock in the 1980s and 1990s. With a set of old-time, rabbit-ear antennae atop the TV, we could usually pick up four channels out of Duluth. On Saturday nights, *The Lawrence Welk Show* was typically no match for a televised University of Minnesota-Duluth Bulldogs hockey game. In 1986, we purchased one of those early VHS tape players. But to rent movies, we had to drive fifty miles to Duluth. I spent some of these quieter days drawing.

The product of a quiet weekend afternoon in winter

I had been pretty good at scientific illustrating of artifacts in my earlier career as an archaeologist, and that skill became handy as my interest in drawing pictures of wildlife at the lighthouse grew. Using pen and ink, I would stipple a design with thousands of small ink dots. It was as close as I ever came to the pastime of those old light keepers who built ships in bottles.

~~~

WE ALWAYS LOOKED forward to the Thanksgiving and Christmas holidays. During our early years at Split Rock in the 1980s, we were a young
family and, like most people, we were anxious to spend the holidays with
our parents and siblings. We loaded up the car with the kids, the dog, the
presents, and the food and spent a few days making the sojourn south.
For me, that meant the Twin Cities, two hundred miles away. Jane's
family was another two hours west in Willmar, Minnesota. The trips
found us driving a big slick and icy loop to see both sides of the family in
one expedition. As our kids grew, these trips became less eagerly anticipated and more dreaded. We began to question ourselves. Wouldn't it
be better to hold a family celebration in July? We felt that our home at

Christmas at the lighthouse,
about 1995

the lighthouse would be the ideal place to spend the holidays, but family pressures always won out.

This came to a head when the kids were about six and four years old. The Christmas trip that year to my folks was a white-knuckle drive in a freezing snowstorm that took six hours instead of the usual four. Once we finally got the kids to bed on Christmas Eve, Jane asked me to fetch their presents from the car so we could place them under the tree in the living room.

I came back in from the car and asked her, "You packed the presents, right?"

She said, "Nooo, I thought you did."

We made the best of a high-anxiety situation, rounding up and wrapping some of the old toys tucked away at my parents' house from my childhood with my siblings. Our wonderful kids seemed a little put out but thankful to open a used G.I. Joe drawing set and some Barbie clothes. Their real gifts sat in a big bag right by the door in our kitchen at home at the lighthouse. When we returned the day after Christmas, I stalled the kids out in the yard while Jane ran into the house and placed the presents under our Christmas tree.

From that year on, we all figured that as long as Santa came to the lighthouse anyway, we should stay home for Christmas. We explained to our parents and siblings that we would be starting our own family tradition by celebrating Christmas at Split Rock. We loved spending most Christmases in our home, surrounded by the peace and tranquility of the north—complete with real snow-covered spruce and fir trees and the glittering open waters of Lake Superior. The four of us hiked across Highway 61 and felled a Christmas tree from where the young spruce and balsam grew in the powerline right-of-way along the highway. With the tree decorated in the living room, and with festive lights and garland throughout the house, our lighthouse home was the coziest place to spend Christmas.

~~~

THE NIGHT SKIES OF WINTER were miracles to behold. Some evenings, when the nights were calm, I left work at the visitor center and took a short detour on my way to the house. I climbed the steps to the observation deck skirting the lighthouse. To the south and east, there was little light pollution, and the sky was inky black over Lake Superior. The winter sky was so different from a warm summer night. Summer stars looked warm and yellow and close enough to touch; winter stars appeared cold and silver and far away. They seemed to crackle and flicker in the brittle air—crystal clear, with all the constellations standing out. In the distance over the calm lake water, I glimpsed faint bubbles of light glowing above the horizon from Two Harbors, Duluth, and Superior. Some nights, a pale glow was visible above Bayfield, Wisconsin, some thirty-seven miles away over the hills of the South Shore. It disappointed me to see the lights of man growing brighter. Since the 1980s, the glow from Two Harbors and Duluth, and even Silver Bay, continued to expand and push back the clear, dark night skies. But on those really dark nights, the skies turned black as coal. The only light came from the stars turning in the heavens, an ore boat heading down the lake off Devils Island, or an occasional satellite cutting a straight line across the sky.

The night chill crept up quickly, but more than once as I turned to head back down the twenty-two steps from the observation deck the silent and unmoving green-white glow of the northern lights caught my eye off in the distance. The green glow shimmered across the northern sky, beyond the little inland towns of Finland and Isabella and past the Boundary Waters Canoe Area and the Canadian border. Sometimes, northern lights strengthen and pulse southward, putting on a flickering and flashing show of billowing green, yellow, or even red curtains of solar energy high in the sky over the lighthouse. But on many winter nights, they stayed near the North Pole—only a ghostly suggestion of what they could be. The glow in the sky looked as if there were a huge gleaming metropolis far to the north.

〜〜〜

NEIGHBORS

In our first years at the lighthouse, we had several neighbors who lived along Highway 61 between Gold Rock Point and the Split Rock River—the area that later became part of Split Rock Lighthouse State Park. In the 1980s and 1990s, five families lived in homes between Chapin's (later Shipwreck) Creek and the old Split Rock Trading Post. The latter, a tourist shop, stood next to the scenic overlook, a highway pull-off offering a sweet view of the lighthouse in the distance. The trading post store featured a lookout tower at the back. For a small charge, you could climb the tower and get an even better view of the lake and lighthouse. About a half mile up the road, Lyle and Rose Shepersky raised a family in a small white house across the highway from where the scuba divers now park for their swims out to the *Madeira* shipwreck.

Across the highway, down by the shore of the lake on Lighthouse Bay, we met a wonderful retired couple, Ray and Esther Jensen. Their place started out as a ma-and-pa resort with five small rustic cabins, put up when the highway was first built in the 1920s. In the late 1970s, when Ray retired from his job as a milkman in the Twin Cities, he and Esther bought the place and moved to the North Shore. Ray did a fantastic job fixing up the cabins. Jane and I got to know many of their relatives and friends who came to visit over the years. One reason Ray and Esther purchased the property was the well that provided good-tasting water—not always a given along the North Shore. The bedrock was another factor. Their own cabin stood just a few feet from the spot where the highest waves crashed during storms, and there was no reason to worry about erosion anytime soon. Ray,

Esther, and the cabins are long gone, but the beautiful little spot is now in the state park—accessible with a short hike from the Gitchi-Gami State Trail.

Another neighbor, Clyde Amundson, lived alone in a small gray house on the north side of the highway about a quarter mile southwest of the state park entrance. For several years, Clyde's wife, Jane, had worked at the historic site as a summer tour guide. Jane and I never got to meet her. She died of cancer the summer before we moved to Split Rock. The lighthouse staff spoke highly of Jane, describing her as a dynamo and an asset to the historic site. Clyde was a quiet, unassuming guy in his eighties when we met him. He had worked for the DNR, supervising crews that built all of the stone retaining walls along the cliff edges near the lighthouse in the early 1970s. I learned so much from Clyde about the country around Split Rock, an area in which he had been deer hunting for years. He pointed out where the old logging camps once stood and where the logging railroad grades ran through the hills behind the state park.

Just west of Clyde's place, there was still a red cabin—the lone private dwelling left within the boundaries of the state park. It belonged to Carl Sannes, a quiet, friendly man whose house stood above the small, No Name Creek valley. His family had lived along the North Shore since around 1910, when Split Rock Lighthouse was built. Carl's parents had sold some land across the highway from his cabin to light keeper Franklin Covell. Covell and his wife, Edith, planned to build a place and live near the lighthouse when he retired as head keeper in 1944. But shortly after he retired, Edith grew ill, and the Covells moved back to Michigan, where their family lived. Around

1950, the Candlelight Motel went up on this land and existed until the early 1970s, when the state purchased the property and the DNR tore it down. In 2020, a new park road to a new campground on the upper side of the highway was built right through the last of the old motel's foundations.

Just west of No Name Creek, on the upper side of the highway, Ed Swarmer and his wife lived in a small wood frame house. Ed took care of his ailing wife at home until she passed away in the early 1980s. I got to know Ed well. He was a good car mechanic with a nice shop in his garage. He made many repairs on the aging cars Jane and I drove. I loved to sit and visit with him in his garage while he turned his wrench and turned back the clock. Ed told me that he was in his early twenties back in the 1920s when he rented a room from my grandparents in Duluth. Feeding deer became Ed's passion, as a large herd wintered in the state park near his house. One of the deer became so tame, I once watched Ed hold a cookie in his teeth while the deer gently took it right out of his mouth. In the winter, hundreds of deer from farther inland came down along the lakeshore to "yard up" because the weather was milder and the snow less deep. The locals who drove back and forth on Highway 61 in the winter learned to watch for deer crossing the highway to get to Ed's feeders.

A few hundred feet west of Ed's place, Gilbert and Joann Pierce made their home. He worked at Reserve Mining for years and she was a nurse at Lakeview Hospital in Two Harbors. About a month after Jane and I arrived at Split Rock, Joann called to invite us to a neighborhood Christmas party at their house. We hadn't met any of the neighbors, and Joann said this would be a good chance to get acquainted. I'm sure they were just as curious about the new couple at the lighthouse as we were about them. We crowded into their house with all the neighbors for a nice gathering featuring good food and Christmas cookies. Jane and I came away from that first party with a warm feeling about our new home and neighbors. Gilbert had a shooting range behind his house, and he invited me to come over and target shoot whenever I wanted. As our kids arrived and grew up, Joann invited all of us over for sledding parties behind their house—one of the area's few hills not covered with forest trees.

The Sve family were the next neighbors to the southwest, about two miles down the highway and on the west side of Split Rock River. The family had lived here since the 1920s—starting out as commercial fishermen. Later, when the highway was built, they started a charter sport-fishing business and built Split Rock Cabins to accommodate the anglers. They would take their guests out on the lake in their cabin cruiser boat, the *Tern*. At that first Christmas party at Gilbert and Joann's home in 1982, I met Ragnvald and Ragnhild Sve, and their two sons, Walter and Leonard, and their wives, Carol and Audrey. The elder Sves came from Norway to settle on the North Shore and retained their thick Norwegian accents. Their sons, and at least one of their grandsons, Eric, still held commercial fishing licenses—rowing out to tend herring nets.

In our last years at the lighthouse, our nearest neighbors lived more than a mile away, toward Beaver Bay. And by 2021, the Sves and Split Rock Cabins were all that remained of our neighbors and their homes. All the rest were willing sellers of their land to the state when the park was expanded and the Minnesota Department of Transportation widened Highway 61 through the state park in 2011.

WE WERE THANKFUL for the few birds that stayed for the long winter. We especially appreciated the ravens' intelligence. Most people are used to seeing common crows, who are likely smart but usually more annoying than intriguing. The raven is the crow's much larger cousin, and for years I had seen them on trips north to the Boundary Waters. But I never lived near ravens until we moved to Split Rock. They are extremely hardy, and I have always been impressed to see them fly high in a clear blue sky when it's twenty below zero in January.

Perky little black-capped chickadees and nuthatches were also willing to stick around all winter and visit our feeder. As long as open water remained, bald eagles spent most of the winter along the North Shore. It was always a welcome sight to see them floating on the wind currents high above the lighthouse. Both ravens and eagles benefited from all the road-kill deer on Highway 61. Ravens scavenging a deer carcass in the ditch, while a pair of bald eagles patiently waited, became a recurring winter scene along the highway. In late winter, with food scarce, we watched from our living room windows as the grouse tightrope-walked far out on the small birch branches growing over the cliff edge to eat the catkins.

~~~

AS KIDS GROWING UP at the lighthouse, John and Anna loved winter. There was always plenty of snow in which to play, sometimes too much— but I never saw it snow as hard and fast as the Halloween snowstorm of 1991. The kids were young, dressed in their Halloween costumes, ready to head to Silver Bay for the children's Halloween party at the Reunion Hall. The snow started falling in the late afternoon and dusk came early. On the way to town, we stopped at the home of our nearest neighbors and good friends, Ray and Esther Jensen, to trick or treat and show off the kids' costumes. They lived nearby along the lakeshore in Lighthouse Bay.

We drove down the steep driveway to their house in our Ford Taurus wagon before we realized how quickly the snow was accumulating. A princess costume was not appropriate winter wear, so after a brief visit with the Jensens, I had to carry five-year-old Anna back to the car. We barely made it up the hill to the highway in our front-wheel drive Taurus without getting stuck. Jane and I knew that discretion was the best idea, so we turned back to the safety of home. Much to the disappointment of John and

The kids' snowmen grew along with them.

Anna, it was too risky to chance the eight-mile drive into Silver Bay. We played games with the kids, throwing our own intimate party. Before bed, I put on my parka and walked outside. The lake snow was coming down in flakes the size of quarters and a foot of snow had already fallen. The storm lasted two days. When it ended on November 2, there was more than three feet of snow on the ground. The winter of 1991–92 was a long one.

When you live on a windswept, exposed rocky point, winter storms are exciting and imposing. The storms came in so many flavors, we learned to read the unpredictable weather. Sometimes they came in as sloppy, slushy nor'easters with howling wind lasting several days. Those were the worst, because of the damage they brought. At other times, a gentle breeze started coming in off the lake with its moisture-laden air, and the lake-effect snow machine began coating the North Shore. We could sometimes see a wall of snow heading toward the lighthouse from out on the lake, and the fluffy snow piled up inches deep in minutes.

Once, Jane bundled up John and Anna so they could play outside in the yard. They were outside only a few minutes when she noticed flakes beginning to fall and looked out on the lake as an ominous wall of snow approached the shore. She quickly ran outside and called to the kids, who were already lost in the heavy snowfall. She was able to guide them back to the house by calling to them until Anna's bright pink snowsuit emerged through the thick, swirling snow.

Some years were much snowier than others, but one hundred inches of snow typically fell each winter. Our pets spent most of their winters inside the house with us. During our thirty-six years at Split Rock, we owned three golden retrievers and a yellow Lab—Ozzie, Dolly, Captain, and Shamus. Dolly, one of the goldens, had fur as thick as a yak's. She often preferred to lie out in the yard during snowstorms until she was nearly covered with snow.

The dogs grew used to visitors touring the lighthouse on the other side of the four-foot-high chain-link fence that surrounded our yard. There were some winters when the snow drifted high enough to completely cover the fence. It was funny how all the dogs climbed up on the snowdrifts, but they knew to stay in the yard and stop where the fence lay deeply buried in snow.

Anna had a calico cat named Frieda. The frisky little feline usually had enough sense to stay in the house during the winter. One unusually warm day in February, she slipped out the door and enjoyed the nice weather.

Lake-effect snow, 2014

That night she failed to come home and the thermometer dropped to minus twenty. Anna was beside herself with worry, so I went out looking for Frieda. First I checked in the storage barns, then on the trails around the lighthouse and down near the lake. She didn't return the next day or the next. A cold snap kept the temperatures below zero that week. On the evening of the fourth day, just as Jane was gently telling Anna that Frieda could not have survived in that cold, I heard a tapping at the living room window. Sure enough, there was Frieda sitting on the sill in the dark— pleading to come in. She appeared none the worse for wear. We always wondered where she could have spent those four subzero days and nights, surrounded by foxes, coyotes, and owls always looking for a meal.

OPPOSITE: Captain parked himself on a snowdrift right at the fence line.

~~~

THE RIVERS OF THE NORTH SHORE held a special enchantment in the winter. I always looked forward to snow-covered rapids and frozen waterfalls. Exploring the Split Rock River was especially fun. By January, the river froze except for spots where the current ran fast. The snows deepened enough that we could cross-country ski right up the river. In the 1980s, people rarely visited the upper reaches of the river—only a few trout fishermen ventured in summer to the pools far upriver. It was always an adventure and an accomplishment to be the first to cross-country ski up the river over the many frozen rapids. Some of those rapids were steep, and we had to herringbone up those portions, huffing and puffing. It took some nerve and experimentation to find the right route up the frozen river. We could hear fast water flowing below the snow and ice, and in places open pools of water were visible.

At least once a winter, I got together with Paul Sundberg, the park manager at Gooseberry Falls, and we skied up the Split Rock River about three miles. We packed our cameras and a small lunch along in our backpacks and snapped pictures of the remote river canyons, rock formations, and animal tracks. We stopped for a snack at the point where the river really starts to drop on its way to Lake Superior. Then the fun began as we let gravity propel us, sailing back down the tracks we had carved coming up the river. An upriver trip that took us three or four hours turned into an exhilarating half-hour ski back down to the lake.

In the late 1980s, a loop of the Superior Hiking Trail was completed—

running up one side of the river canyon about two miles, crossing the river on a foot bridge, and coming down the other side of the river back to the wayside parking lot at the river's mouth. Since then, hundreds of hikers, skiers, and snowshoers have discovered and explored the trail's river loop.

By the late 1990s, the winter river became the frigid playground of trekkers. Once the river froze and snow fell, snowshoers and skiers established a well-packed trail up the lower river about a half mile to the first waterfall.

Over the years, Paul and I took several ski trips up and down many of the North Shore rivers. Once we threw our skis in a car, drove up behind Beaver Bay, and took County Road 3 past the Silver Bay airport to where the road passed over the Split Rock River. From there, we skied downhill about nine miles back to the wayside rest at the mouth of the river where we had left a car. We were always looking for downhill routes to ski. Who wants to ski uphill if you don't have to? And the river gorges afforded such fantastic scenery. Paul, myself, and a couple of other friends repeated the practice on the Cascade River, parking a car on Cook County Road 45, skiing down the river about five miles, and ending back at the river mouth. The Devil Track River also provided a great route to ski up the gorge from Highway 61 until we reached a waterfall a few miles upriver. That waterfall, when frozen, has become popular with ice climbers.

The steep gradients of the rivers flowing into the lake also offered plenty of fun in the late winter. Over ledges where waterfalls roar in the summer, only a trickle of water flows in wintertime. The river water continues to flow and freeze over these ledges. By March, it begins to look like someone has poured a giant root beer float down the river and it froze. I put cleats on over my boots and climbed the frozen falls up the river—for powerful river views and access to gorges you just don't see in the summer.

Lake Superior continues to cool as winter progresses, with ice usually forming on the lake by mid-February or early March. Often, on a cold, calm night, the surface began to freeze, and by morning we found an inch

John snowshoes on the Split Rock River, 2003.

OPPOSITE: Wolf tracks on the Split Rock River, 2018

A frozen waterfall on Split Rock Creek, 2010

or two of ice on the lake. The lake was always moving; even on a perfectly calm twenty-below-zero morning, there were small undulations of rolling water under the ice. The surface ice was thin and flexible enough to roll with the movement of the water. We called it rubber ice. As this ice thickened, it lost its flexibility, and the rolling lake broke it up into so-called pancake ice. These were perfectly circular pieces of ice floating on the surface. Sometimes, if a wind came up, the pancake ice was blown in to shore and piled up in huge ridges of ice shards. About once a decade, several days of cold, calm weather caused the lake to freeze as smooth as a freshly Zamboni-ed hockey rink as far out as we could see. One year

Newly frozen ice—a perfect
natural skating rink, 2005

when the lake froze smooth with no snow, John and I grabbed our skates and hockey sticks and ran down to the shoreline. The conditions were perfect. Sitting on the concrete slab of the pump house foundation, we laced up our skates for a rare chance to skate on the mirror-smooth ice of Lake Superior. As we skated, we looked down through the ice to see huge boulders on the lake bottom as it dropped off fifty feet and beyond. We used small rocks from the lakeshore as hockey pucks and shot them out over the smooth ice. They kept gliding for hundreds of yards.

In our early years at the lighthouse, there were more winters when the lake froze as far as we could see and then stayed frozen for weeks. The sounds of the lake shift as conditions change. For most of the year, when the lake is ice-free, we heard the constant gurgling, splashing, or whispering of the water moving among the rocks and gravel on the shoreline. On windier days, we heard the crashing of waves. When the lake froze over, the only noise we heard were occasional booms and groans of ice shifting and cracking. Some of these booms started below the lighthouse and traveled for miles as new cracks formed. The rumble traveled way out over the lake—sometimes waking us from a sound sleep. When the lake froze, we sometimes saw wolves or coyotes traveling out on the ice. I once watched a lone timber wolf loping out from the shoreline, following him with binoculars until he became a distant black dot on the white ice heading straight across the lake toward the Wisconsin shore.

In March or April, when the ice is breaking up, especially distinctive sounds come from the ice, wind, and currents. In the coves and bays along the shore the ice freezes first and thickest, then stays in place the longest. Beyond the points of land, the ice breaks loose and the whole ice surface starts to move down the shoreline. With the right wind, this shelf ice can move faster than a man can walk. When it rubs up against the ice shelf anchored to shore, it peels off an array of icy shards. Some look like thin window glass, while other chunks can be eight inches thick. The ice sheet moves for miles, rubbing against the shoreline ice to create ever-changing sounds. I will never forget standing next to Lake Superior and witnessing this breakup. I could hear the tinkling of bells or a deep roar of grinding ice as it piled up in windrows.

Snow removal became a large part of my winter work in the early years. We added a full-time maintenance man the last twenty years to lighten

Some years the lake froze over completely, as in 2009.

my load. But he lived twenty miles away, while I was on site. So the bigger the storm, the better the chance that we were on our own to gain access to the highway. The worst snowstorms were the blizzards that brought bitter winds and up to two feet of snow. Drifts piled up, so we needed snowshoes just to get from the house to the garage, tractor, and snowblower. On those days, I started long before daylight, piloting the site's tractor to plow out the main roads and paths. Then we waited for state snowplows to clear the road to the highway. The plow drivers had all of Highway 61 to clean, so we were a low priority. Sometimes we waited days before they reached us.

〜〜

WITH THE ADVENT OF digital photography, it seemed that everyone had
become a photographer. Even on winter days, more and more people
made their way to the lighthouse to take pictures. Having to deal with
people driving into the historic site before roads were plowed became one
of my pet peeves. They tromped up to the lighthouse, packing down the
snow before I could clear at least a narrow path for them. Several times,
I helped shovel out their cars stuck in unplowed snow in the parking lot.
After a storm, I started before daylight, first shoveling the twenty-two
steps to the observation deck beside the base of the lighthouse. During
nor'easters, giant snow drifts formed right along the fence at the cliff edge
near the fog signal building, burying the fence and increasing the danger
of a fall. Photographers gravitated to this spot. It was always a contest to
see if I could clear the deck before they packed the snow with their boots.

I attacked the drifts with a scoop shovel—spending a couple of hours throwing shovels full of snow over the cliff side and into the lake below. If an updraft blew up the cliff face, it would puff the fine, fluffy snow right back up the cliff. Don't get me wrong, I loved those moments and often paused to catch my breath in the crisp air—overlooking one of the greatest views on earth. Once I cleared the observation deck, I jumped back on the tractor and plowed the rock-hard drifts from the footpath to the lighthouse.

Some of the nastiest winter storms come in late March, or even into mid-April. Like finales at fireworks shows, it seemed like every winter tried to put up one last blast of defiance before surrendering to a tentative spring. This final storm usually packed a combination of screaming wind, thick snow, and freezing rain. You better be where you need to be because ice coated the roads, power lines, and anything or anyone caught outdoors. In March 2009, an overnight ice storm put down a half inch of ice,

Shoveling the
observation deck

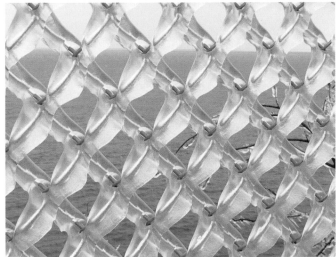

shutting down Highway 61, closing local schools, and prompting power outages. All day, we heard the snapping and cracking of broken branches from the weight of the ice on the trees. Ten years later, birch trees with missing branches told the tale around the historic site.

Walking to get the mail was one of my favorite treks. Winters challenged my wherewithal to maintain this daily half-mile hike from my office in the visitor center to the mailboxes on Highway 61 at the entrance road to the state park. There were three mailboxes, one for the Radzak family, one for the historic site, and one for the state park. I picked up our personal mail and delivered any to the historic site. I often grabbed the DNR's mail for the state park and dropped it off at the park office, which gave me an opportunity to share any news with the park staff.

Winter traffic up the hill into the state park was light, which was most appreciated when the snowbanks piled high and the road narrowed. I bundled up in my parka, strapped my ice cleats over my boots, threw my mailbag over my shoulder, and slipped on my chopper mittens. It was just shy of a mile round trip to the highway and back, but if the north wind blew straight up the park road, it felt like ten miles. When fresh snow dusted the ground, I checked the tracks to see which animals had been making the rounds overnight.

I noticed their tracks before I saw the doe and her two fawns, usually crossing the road or off in the trees. Every morning there were new coyote or fox tracks, and I saw where they had hunted snowshoe hare. One day in early April, after a late-season snowstorm, I came across an odd trail that looked like a fat snake had slid through the snow, then got up on its feet and run for a few yards before taking another long slide. I realized it was

Ice storm, 2009

Ice coats the chain-link fence, 2009.

an otter running and sliding through the snow. I wondered what an otter was doing up on top of the cliff far from the lakeshore.

Getting the mail wasn't always routine or dull. Highway 61 can be an icy, treacherous road in the winter. For cars traveling north from Two Harbors, the route slopes downhill and provides a short right turn lane to the state park. Once, as I approached the mailboxes, walking past the stop sign for the park road, I did not see a guy in a Subaru Outback turning into the park from the highway. Just as I passed the stop sign, he slid off the intersection and skidded into the ditch. I never saw him until I heard him crash into the stop sign about ten feet behind me. On another snowy day, I was retrieving the mail and standing at the boxes with my back to the highway. The UPS truck was just coming down the hill from making deliveries at the visitor center. At the stop sign, I noticed the driver pointing behind me. I spun around in time to see a car that was just passing me, swerving wildly on the icy road. It slid into the ditch about fifty yards down the highway. I ran down the shoulder to check on the car's occupants. A lone young woman got out—badly shaken up but fine. Her car was hung up on some rocks in the ditch and couldn't be driven. I invited her to walk back with me to the visitor center, where we could call for help. That was a lucky one for all of us.

On another trip to the mailbox, this time in the summer, I was confronted by a guy in his thirties with hair as wild as his eyes. He pulled over near me and jumped out of his car, wearing only gym shorts. He came at me with what appeared to be ill intent, flailing his arms and shouting incoherently. I stood my ground but prepared for some evasive maneuvering. After what seemed like an eternity, with no one else stopping to assist, the wild man jumped back in his beater of a car and took off in the direction of Two Harbors. I hightailed it up the hill to the nearest phone at the state park office, called 911, and described the car and the man to the Lake County Sheriff's department. I later learned that the county sheriff and deputies spotted him near Gooseberry Falls, where he spun around and headed northeast up the highway. Using tire deflation spikes thrown out on the highway, they caught him near Little Marais. He was high on something, had a warrant out for his arrest, and ended up in the county jail.

~~~

AS THE SEASONS CHANGE, winter always lasts long this far north, but inevitably and grudgingly it gives in to spring. Slowly, day by day, the sun climbs higher and the air warms, at least at midday. By early May, most of the snow has disappeared. When the kids were young and the weather warm, they enjoyed a stroller ride to the mailbox with Jane and me. It was always much easier going to the highway than pushing a stroller loaded with two toddlers back up the hill to the cliff top. Shamus the dog always wanted to come along on the walks to the mailbox. The spring air was perfume to me. To Shamus, it was an intoxicating aroma of freshly exposed earthy odors. We also had a cat that was convinced she was a dog. When the snow finally melted, she followed Shamus and me all the way to the mailbox and back. People passing by on the park road would chuckle, seeing a guy being led by a big dog and followed by a fat cat that looked a lot like a raccoon.

Seen on the way to the mailbox, January 2012

June 2013.
Paul Sundberg Photography

3.
≈ *Spring* ≈

Spring is a state of mind on the North Shore of Lake Superior. Meteorologists say spring starts March 1. Astronomers pick March 20 as its start because of the vernal equinox, when the sun passes back north over the equator and shines down from the northern hemisphere every day for the next six months. But north of Duluth, no matter what the calendar says, March does not mean spring. Not with three feet of snow in the woods and a lake full of ice.

Spring comes to Split Rock in little hints and whispers. You feel its approach in the strength of the sun and the way the snow melts from the trails on a sunny day. You see it in the shortening shadow of the lighthouse at noon, as the sun rides higher in the sky. You sense the daylight growing four minutes longer every day. Ravens nest and gulls and bald eagles return to patrol the shoreline. And, best of all, by the last week in March, the Soo Locks at the eastern end of Lake Superior open for the shipping season. Nothing says "spring" on the North Shore like ore boats once again passing by on the big lake. Most years, a surprise blizzard blows in around the second week in April. But those spring snowstorms are almost laughable. We know they're winter's last gasp.

≈

MARCH AND APRIL are a time of anticipation and preparation at the Split Rock historic site. Energy flows again in all directions. Every spring, I felt the pressure build to ready the site for another busy season. Preparing the staff, the buildings and grounds, and the interpretive program for the upcoming tourism season all began elbowing for room on my to-do list. In March there were trips to St. Paul to visit state legislators at the capitol, plus more meetings with local tourism and marketing groups. We juggled all that each spring, getting ready to open the site.

To keep the site open for nine hours every day in the *continued on page 84*

TOURISM THROUGH THE YEARS

Today, Split Rock ranks as one of the most visited historic sites in the state and the most popular destination among tourists along Minnesota's shoreline of Lake Superior. It makes you wonder if the US Lighthouse Service chose the location because of its beauty and majesty.

As the light station prepared to open in 1910, the *Duluth Herald* ran a short article with a photograph of the cliff-top lighthouse and predicted that it would become a popular tourist destination. The paper made this prediction even though, back then, boats provided the only access to the lighthouse. Early light keepers mentioned people visiting the station. First assistant keeper Harry Thompson noted two lighthouse visitors in his journal on June 12, 1913. Another eighteen people stopped by on June 29, 1913, and some North Shore neighbors from Castle Danger were among the ten visiting on August 3, 1913. These early visits would have been pretty informal affairs as many of the visitors were commercial fishermen or neighbors who the keepers knew.

More than a decade passed before the road along the North Shore was completed past Split Rock in the autumn of 1924. Two Harbors and Beaver Bay were finally connected on a direct route along the shore that passed a half mile from the lighthouse. When the road was designated as part of US Highway 61 in 1926, Duluth tourism groups began to promote the lighthouse as a destination, along with the falls on the Gooseberry and Cascade Rivers and the Gunflint Trail. (The state parks would be established later.) "Split Rock Light and Horn Guard Against Storm and Fog; Tourists Love the Place," a *Duluth Herald* headline proclaimed in June 1926. The article said, "tourists by the thousands will visit the great Split Rock light and its environment this year." Word was getting out that Split Rock was a must-see on an excursion up the North Shore.

By the early 1930s, Split Rock head keeper Franklin Covell was blowing more than fog warnings. He began expressing concern to Lighthouse Service honchos in Detroit about juggling swarms of tourists while trying to operate the lighthouse and foghorn. Covell estimated that a total of five thousand people visited the lighthouse in June 1935. With the station open to tourists from sunrise to sunset every day except Sunday, Covell counted an average of forty-one daily visitors. His wife, Edith, complained about tourists peeking in the windows of their house and picking the flowers that she had worked so hard to grow along the sidewalk just beyond their front porch. When Covell finally requested a fence around

ABOVE: Tourists on the dock at Little Two Harbors in the 1940s. *MNHS*
OPPOSITE: Lake Superior International Highway tourist brochure, 1926. *MNHS*

the three keepers' homes, his Eleventh District lighthouse superintendent in Detroit said, "No." Instead, he was told to put up signs instructing visitors to stay on sidewalks.

Lighthouse traffic escalated in 1936. Workers in the Depression-era Civilian Conservation Corps had built a road the previous summer to the light station from the highway. Now lighthouse visitors could park nearby—no more half-mile walk from the highway.

Braced for an uptick in visitors, Lighthouse Service bosses in Detroit bolstered the Split Rock workforce, adding Gardar O. Pedersen as an additional assistant keeper to help with the night watches. The

hiring freed up Covell and the first assistant keeper to "permit the proper handling of visitors during the tourist season," according to a letter dated July 9, 1936, from Fred P. Dillon, the superintendent of lighthouses for the Eleventh District of the Lighthouse Service in Detroit.

The superintendent made it clear the light keeper and his first assistant were expected to "assume the principal responsibility of receiving and guiding visitors through the station, showing them the facilities and equipment during the hours that the station is open to visitors." Lighthouse Service regulations required those keepers to greet visitors in official uniforms. The dress

107-D Split Rock Lighthouse, 200 Feet Above Beautiful Lake Superior

TOP: Postcard, about 1945. *MNHS;* ABOVE: Terry and G. T. Amell, grandchildren of first assistant keeper Tom Hassing, about 1949. *Courtesy G. T. Amell;* OPPOSITE: A busy summer day, 2016

PLEASE
KEEP OFF
THE GRASS

code became necessary to differentiate the employees from the hordes of visitors. Covell wrote to his superiors that 23,600 visitors signed the register book in the lighthouse in July, August, and September in the mid-1930s—and he estimated that only one-third of the visitors signed the guest books.

The Lighthouse Service's public relations savvy rivaled its ability to keep boats safe on the lakes. That 1936 letter from Detroit headquarters instructed Covell to keep in touch with the tourist agencies in Duluth and Superior and advertise the visiting hours at Split Rock Light Station. Keepers should "cultivate the good will of the general public in every way practicable," Dillon wrote to Covell. Split Rock had suddenly become a "show" station for the government. In 1939, the Lighthouse Service published a promotional booklet listing Split Rock among the ten best-known lighthouses in the country—calling it "one of the most frequently visited lighthouses in the United States."

By the time the US Coast Guard took over responsibility for the nation's lighthouses in 1939, keepers and their families could only look back with nostalgia to the quiet life at Split Rock. The Coast Guard kept the civilian keepers on the job, but they now faced visitors at all hours. Years later, Keeper Covell's children recalled how tourists occasionally walked in on them in their own house. They remembered seeing their mother in tears over people picking her roses. Thanks to World War II, the lighthouse families got a break. The light station was closed to visitors for security reasons from 1941 to 1945. During the war, Covell asked to be issued a .45-caliber handgun to help him keep the station safe. Coast Guard officials in Cleveland turned down his request.

Visitors returned at high levels after the war. Although wartime advancements in navigational technology and new equipment at Silver Bay made Split Rock Light Station obsolete by the late 1950s, the Coast Guard kept it open and operational through the late 1960s, partly because of the high tourism traffic. The light station was decommissioned in 1969 and stood empty until 1971, but still the tourists kept coming. In the summer of 1971, it reopened as a Minnesota state park. New amenities were added to serve the ever-growing number of visitors. The Minnesota Historical Society has operated the light station as a state historic site since 1976—adding to the tour program and making the historic buildings more accessible. By 1990, the number of annual visitors soared to 212,365 between mid-May and mid-October. That added up to 1,300 people per day. Annual visitation stabilized at about 160,000 visitors after 1990s fee, tour times, and open hours adjustments to reduce crowding and overuse.

During my years as the site's manager, the staff and I welcomed more than four million visitors to Split Rock Lighthouse.

height of the summer season, we had around thirty-four people on staff
each year. We needed fourteen people who could work as guides, taking
three tour groups of up to fifty people through the site every hour. Staffing the visitor center museum store called for another ten employees, plus
two maintenance people. Most of these people worked part-time. By the
late 1990s, the operation had grown so large that we added an interpretive
program manager, a museum store manager, an administrative assistant,
and a facilities maintenance man, all working full-time. As with any small
but growing business, there were challenges. I was always grateful for the
quality and dedication of the staff. Many returned year after year to work
at the site from May through October. Each year we hired about five new
people, as some staff moved on to other things. Many were college stu-
dents or retired teachers. Each spring the interviewing and hiring process
was a big job, and my full-time staff and I were always impressed at the
excellent caliber of the applicants. The people we hired were all troup-
ers to make it through a whole summer welcoming and talking to and
answering many of the same questions from around a thousand people
every day, all summer and into the fall. As their supervisor, I was the one
they came to for solutions to problems. Complaints or misbehavior from

Interpreters Alex Helland (posing) and Ed Maki Jr. (on steps) help visitors at the lighthouse, 2011.

OPPOSITE: During the annual children's day event in 2005, volunteer Laura Ryan demonstrates how to do laundry, while interpreter Denise Carlson (on blanket) shares crafts of the 1920s.

visitors were exceedingly rare, but on occasion the staff would experience them, and it was my policy to respond to all complaints personally and take any heat or resolve the problem, not push that responsibility to the guides or sales staff.

Then we needed to carve out time for the repair and maintenance of buildings and grounds, preparing them for the thousands of visitors we knew were coming. Fortunately, by the late 1980s, the swelling number of guests and the new visitor center enabled me to hire a full-time maintenance person to help shoulder the year-round load of work required. It seemed like winters grew shorter than they used to be. More and more people ventured out and traveled each spring. Keeping the visitor center open through the winter helped increase these numbers after 2000. We once waited until mid-May to prepare, opening the lighthouse for the summer on May 15. By 2017, Opening Day moved up to March 1 to accommodate the growing number of spring visitors. Despite those winter and spring upturns, half the people who visit the lighthouse each year do so during July and August.

A FRIENDLY VISITOR, 1931

In 1931, as the Split Rock Lighthouse turned twenty-one, a writer named Stella M. Champney from the *Detroit News* arrived on the lighthouse tender *Marigold* for a brief visit. She was writing a four-part series titled, "Romance of the Lighthouse Service," and her story on Split Rock would appear in the paper on May 17 under the subheading, "Happy Women Here."

   Edith Covell, the wife of the head lighthouse keeper, became the writer's focus—even though Edith's first name was never used. She was simply referred to as Mrs. Franklin Covell. Edith was born in 1879 in Burlington, Michigan; in 1920, when Frank served as an assistant keeper down the North Shore at Two Harbors, the census listed five children in the family. By 1930, only one child—eleven-year-old Claudia Ileana—was listed as living with the Covells. Here is Stella Champney's 1931 account.

"I'M HAPPY HERE," said Mrs. Franklin J. Covell, wife of the head keeper. "I've got a good husband. We have everything we need. It's nice up here. We like it."

   The Split Rock lighthouse is set on the dizzy heights of a rocky promontory, seemingly inaccessible from the shore. As the lighthouse tender *Marigold* drew nearer one could discern a snubby little concrete dock against the rocks, and leading from it, steps! Steps that followed the tramway over which they carried the freight, a tramway that uses 600 feet of cable. Up, up to the top of the bluff we went, Rover and I, with Mr. Covell panting along. Then up to the top of the tower, where the focal belt [the focused area of light], 178 feet above the lashing seas, flashes its warning across the lake.

   It was sunset, the hour for lighting the lamp. Justus G. Luick, first assistant, was filling the Bunson burner

as we climbed the steps where the great glass hangs. In a few minutes that glorious light was flashing out across the waters, faintly at first, gaining in brilliance as the burner warmed, until its majesty became awe-inspiring.

   "They see the light at Devil's Island," said Mr. Covell. "And we see theirs."

   Down below Adam B. Sayles was watching the power room of the fog signal, cleaning and polishing. In the three residences, back from the bluff, the women were putting away the supper dishes. The *Marigold*, lying at anchor, nodded and swung gently about as the waves rocked her.

   "The wrecks were awful along this shore before the light was built," said Covell. "The magnetic force of the minerals plays with the compass, and pulls ships upon these rocks, unless the mariner can see where he is. It pulled the steamer *Lafayette* ashore and broke her in two, back in 1905. Five years

later they built the lighthouse."

One who has not seen a lighthouse glass cannot form a conception of the beauty. Only in France can be found the rare quality of sand that gives the prisms their clarity and smoothness and softness of effect. All are imported from Paris. An alcohol torch heats the vaporizer, for there is no electricity here, and a 120,000-candle power light flashes every 10 seconds, while the great glass set in a framework of polished brass swings smoothly about clock works run with weights of iron timing it.

"The mercury," said Mr. Covell, "in which the ball bearings rest, cost Uncle Sam $3 a pound. There are 300 pounds in the case here, replenished a few pounds at a time, as it deteriorates."

Split Rock–Devil's Island, crossing lights on the steamer lane. I saw them both, last October, on my way to Superior Entry on the freighter, *John J. Barlum,* flashing their warnings against the rocky, dangerous coasts over which they stand guard.

"It's a pretty light," said Mrs. Covell.

As I turned to go back down the path, down the long, long flight of steps leading to the dock, where the *Marigold's* launch was waiting for me, she grabbed her hat and coat.

"I'll go with you," she said, suppressed eagerness in her voice.

Hands reached out to help me into the boat as soon as we reached the dock. There was no time to visit longer.

"You've got to climb all those steps," I said in parting. "I'm sorry."

The flicker of a smile flashed across her face.

"I climb them once in a while," she said. "I don't mind."

That night, as the *Marigold* swung gently at her anchor and the Split Rock light flashed into my stateroom, the thought of those women up there on the bluff came into my mind. There was something about them that was sweet and wholesome and brave, and a little wistful, it seemed to me.

Split Rock and Devil's Island are more than lights that flash their warnings to mariners of dangerous, rocky coasts.

They are greetings, one to another, of isolated women, sent across the treacherous water of Lake Superior.

SPRING PREPARATION in 1993 packed real excitement. That's when the movie business came to Split Rock—complete with Macaulay Culkin of *Home Alone* fame and Elijah Wood, who had already appeared in a half dozen movies but would become a major star in *The Lord of the Rings* movie series, starting in 2001. Two men showed up in my office in late February, scouting lighthouse locations for a major motion picture. Twentieth Century Fox had sent them from the East Coast to find the perfect cliff location—something that eluded them along the New England coast. We talked about what they needed, the size of the crew, when they wanted to film, and what the film was about.

The film told a story set at an oceanside location in Maine. Surprisingly, they failed to find a tall, vertical cliff anywhere in New England for the final cliffhanger scene in the movie. They were trying to come up with a solution when the director, Joseph Ruben, saw a calendar picture of Split Rock Lighthouse perched on its perfect 130-foot cliff. He immediately sent the two scouts to check it out. They didn't want to use the lighthouse in the movie, just the cliff, with Lake Superior as a stand-in for the Atlantic Ocean. They wanted to film for about two weeks in March—usually a quiet time at the lighthouse. I reminded the movie scouts that Superior is a freshwater lake, and it might be covered with ice at that time. They were willing to take their chances. They planned to build an artificial cliff on top of the real cliff between the fog signal building and the old hoist and derrick site. We were glad their moviemaking wouldn't affect any of our historic buildings. They did need to drill several one-inch diameter holes in the solid anorthosite rock on the cliff top to anchor their scaffolding for the fake cliff. We agreed to allow them to drill the holes but required them to save the rock dust from the holes and mortar it back into place to fill the holes when they were done. We did not want any signs that they had been there or had altered the historic site in any way when they eventually removed their set.

I passed on all the information to my boss at the Minnesota Historical Society in St. Paul. We negotiated a location fee (part of which eventually came to the site) and some amendments to their standard contract, and we both signed.

Twentieth Century Fox wanted to keep the film's plot a secret until it was released. The company's representatives did share its name, its

leading actors, and a quick synopsis with me: *The Good Son* featured two boys—one good and one evil. Wood and Culkin were both twelve years old in 1993. Canadian actress Wendy Crewson played their mother. The acting trio, "the talent," would spend two weeks filming at Split Rock. The film company also received permission to build two additional cliff-top sets on Palisade Head, and another vertical cliff above the lake a dozen miles up the North Shore in Tettegouche State Park.

We were amazed at how much money, time, and effort went into filming for just a few minutes in a major motion picture. They even hired a charter fishing boat captain from nearby Beaver Bay just to drive his boat around in circles so its wake would make the calm lake appear more ocean-like. Eighty cast and crew members spent two weeks building the set and filming the scenes. They shot an additional scene in the birch woods along the trail near the lighthouse tramway ruins. We allowed the crew to eat lunch and warm up in the Split Rock Lighthouse Visitor Center. We smiled at just how cold the crew, mostly Californians, felt in what we considered mild March weather.

Thanks to his *Home Alone* movies, Culkin was a bigger star than Wood in the early 1990s. His star status oozed in all the attention showered on him while filming at Split Rock. When his personal assistant purchased a BB gun for him at the hardware store in Silver Bay, I knew I would have to keep an eye on the young star. The next thing I knew, he was outside the visitor center shooting at red squirrels, birds, or anything that moved—or stood still. I had to play the bad guy, telling him guns were banned and animals protected within state parks and historic sites. Crew members held their breath as I lectured the twelve-year-old. People simply did not address the child star that way. But he was okay with it and put away the BB gun.

Macaulay traveled with his own tutor to provide schooling between scenes. I was asked if I knew a quiet place for them to hold classes, as the commotion at the visitor center was distracting. The other two keeper's houses were out, as they were only heated to forty degrees in the winter. After clearing it with Jane, I volunteered the use of the dining room in our house. Anna and John were five and eight years old at the time. John was at school in Silver Bay during the day, but Anna was home with Jane, and they had to be quiet to not disturb the lessons. Macaulay would study with the teacher for an hour or two and then be called off to shoot another scene, returning in the afternoon for another lesson. John and Anna visited with Macaulay on a couple of occasions, but his time was taken up by the movie and his schooling. I asked both Macaulay and Elijah Wood if they would like to see how a real lighthouse works—leading them up to the lighthouse and letting them wind the weights to make the lens spin. They were both fascinated by the lens and the view from the tower.

Elijah Wood was friendly and outgoing. One afternoon, I brought John and Anna over to see the bustling movie set. Between filming scenes, the

Anna, Elijah Wood, and John

actors had plenty of downtime. Elijah made a point of coming over to visit with John and Anna. They discussed the finer points of Nintendo games. Even at that age, Elijah was captivated by what was going on behind the camera. He talked with camera operators, looking through their lens and asking about different shots and angles.

The lake stayed ice-free and the two weeks the crew spent at Split Rock went smoothly, but at times I wondered if it would ever end. Movie people are absorbed in their craft—they think what they're doing is far more important than anything else going on around them. For example, they wanted to run wires into the historic buildings for electricity. When I told them that was impossible, they accepted it and went out and bought three new portable electric generators.

Macaulay Culkin winds the lighthouse mechanism.

All this fame and activity in March along the North Shore was a shot in the arm for residents and businesses. It's not every day that moviemakers come to town. *The Good Son* came out later in 1993. There was no premiere showing of the film anywhere along the North Shore, despite locals' hopes. In fact, the film never generated much acclaim and soon vanished from theaters. Maybe they should have used the lighthouse in the movie after all.

~~~

PARK AND SITE, TESTING THE PARTNERSHIP

In the early 1990s, a disagreement about money created perhaps the biggest test of the partnership between the Department of Natural Resources and the Minnesota Historical Society at Split Rock. Visitors purchased daily or annual vehicle permits and enjoyed access to everything in the park, including the lighthouse and all its programming. This was also true for the four other historic sites located in state parks. Park fees all went into the DNR's coffers to fund its many needs. The society hadn't charged admission fees for these sites, but with all the improvements and growing visitation at the lighthouse and elsewhere, it was becoming harder to pay for the added staff and programs. The society's administrators went to the state legislature every other year to request operating funds, which were becoming harder to come by. By 1990, the society knew that it needed more money to operate at Split Rock, as well as at other historic sites across the state. The need for more revenue was more pronounced at Split Rock because the old lighthouse attracted more visitors than any other site in the network, including Fort Snelling and

the state capitol. A new deal had to be worked out with the DNR.

In 1991, the Minnesota Historical Society let both the legislature and the DNR know that it would need to start charging admission fees at all historic sites, including those in state parks. The issue proved thorny because, according to Minnesota law, every vehicle entering a state park had to have a vehicle permit. This law needed to be amended, allowing the DNR to waive fees for people who visited only the lighthouse. As expected, the DNR bristled at the notion of losing the revenue it had been collecting from people who weren't visiting the state park.

I had a front-row seat in many meetings, at Split Rock and at both the Minnesota Historical Society and the DNR headquarters in St. Paul. We struggled to work out a solution amenable to both agencies and the public. The society's administrators wished to start charging an admission fee at Split Rock in July 1991. Since the law hadn't been changed, the DNR still needed to charge for park access. If visitors wanted to come onto the lighthouse grounds, they had to pay fees to each agency—not a great solution.

Through that first summer and fall, beginning July 1, 1991, the DNR collected both fees at its contact station. Visitor numbers plummeted, and both the park and the historic site staff fielded complaints from an angry public. The problem was eased during the 1992 legislative session with a new law exempting visitors to Split Rock Lighthouse and other sites within state parks from paying for a state park vehicle permit.

But legislative solutions take time. The new law wouldn't be enacted until July 1, 1992, so Mark Kovacovich, the state park manager, and I scrambled to come up with a workaround. We needed to figure out a way for the society to collect its fees the next May and still follow laws requiring the DNR to charge for vehicle permits through June. We even considered building a separate entrance road to the historic site or moving the state park contact station—anything to combat redundant fee collection. Our solution wasn't elegant, but it worked. Before July 1, the DNR collected the park permit fee from all visitors and the new historic site fee from those who were headed to the site. We sent staff over to help with the work. Once a month, the DNR reimbursed the historical

MINNESOTA HISTORICAL SOCIETY

society for our portion. By the time the new statute kicked in on July 1, saying that the state park fee could be waived to enter the historic site, we worked out another system. The staff at the visitor center would charge for site visits and offer visitors a free pass to tour Split Rock Lighthouse State Park. With new signage and fencing, admission wristbands, and free park passes, it worked pretty well. During the next two years, we worked out the kinks in a system that answered the needs of the DNR, the historical society, the state legislators, and most importantly, the visiting public.

Split Rock Lighthouse Historic Site remains the crown jewel and centerpiece of Split Rock Lighthouse State Park. It's the overwhelming reason most visitors cite for coming to the park. There's pride in knowing that most of those visitors don't even realize that the lighthouse is within the statutory boundary of the state park and the park and historic site are run by different agencies with slightly different missions, both focused on serving the people of the state.

A bobcat stops by for a meal of suet.

BIRDWATCHING became a natural hobby living as close to nature as we did, and spring was high season. When we moved up in 1982, we found an ancient, rickety bird feeder crafted from a log and old wood hanging outside our kitchen window. Over the years, I built new bird feeders—always aiming for bigger and better. I lost count of how many. They lasted until either a bear knocked them down or the voracious red squirrels chewed them up. We once purchased one of those supposedly squirrel-proof metal feeders with a perch that closed if a squirrel put weight on it. It took about three days for the red squirrels to come up with a work-around on that. Back to the drawing board, where my limited woodworking skills were put to the test. One March, we even had a bobcat at the feeder, going after the suet we put out for the birds. He then retired to the porch, to clean himself.

The bird feeder and kitchen window were on the same side of the house as the lighthouse, so that's where tourists walked. It was a great place for a feeder to attract birds, which in turn attracted lighthouse visitors. Our privacy fell right in the mix. If people stopped to watch the birds at the feeder, they were looking right into our kitchen window. When we sat at the kitchen table eating supper, we sensed it when someone looked through binoculars or took pictures across the chain-link fence twenty feet away. They were not taking pictures of us, but that was us in the background of the birds at the feeder.

In the spring, as in the fall, the North Shore serves as a natural flyway for birds migrating along the big lake's rocky coast. All kinds of bird species stopped at our feeder as they passed through. Like so many of our fellow Minnesotans, we eagerly watched for the birds' return each spring. The variety of birds diminished after the 1980s and 1990s.

We kept a journal for several years, recording when different birds showed up. We saw crossbills and three kinds of grosbeaks: pine, evening, and rose-breasted. There were cedar and Bohemian waxwings, redpolls, Baltimore orioles, and the occasional red-winged blackbird making pit stops at our feeder on their spring trips north. Their songs signaled spring's return. Many built nests in the trees near the lighthouse and stayed all summer. White-throated sparrows have a wonderful lilting song that always reminded us of the North Woods. Every year, many phoebes nested in the ninebark and gooseberry bushes in front of our house along the cliff edge. Jane called them squeeze birds because their *fee-bee* call sounded just like someone squeezing a rubber toy—chirps that always made us laugh. We heard, but rarely saw, vireos, ovenbirds, redstarts, and many warblers in the forest around the lighthouse. Ruby-throated hummingbirds were among our favorite summer birds. Around the first of May, when patches of snow still clung in the shadows, we placed three hummingbird feeders just outside the kitchen window. Male hummers would soon show up, followed by the females a week or two later. We always marveled at the great number of tiny

The person with the blonde hair is aiming a camera directly into our kitchen, 2005.

Ravens' nest, 2012

So near, and yet so far,
from the hummingbirds

hummingbirds nesting around the lighthouse and visiting our feeders. By
mid-July, young birds hatched, learned to fly, and joined the adults at the
feeders. Dozens of the tiny, darting birds often vied for space—hovering
and diving at the feeder at the same time. The buzzing and humming of
the iridescent little birds taunted our cat, Harry, as he lurked behind the
window screen—a foot away from the feeders.

For several years, a pair of ravens nested in a notch in the cliff face
below the lighthouse, which we could only see from the stairway to the
lake. One of the ravens came to recognize the dog and me as we made the
rounds on the trails near the lighthouse. He often dipped down as he flew
by and croaked a guttural *wonk-wonk* at us. Ravens playfully rode the rising winds blowing up the face of the cliff. We loved to watch their mock
fighting and tumbling aerobatics. We also got a kick out of the adults
teaching their young fledglings to fly by coaxing them out of the nest.
Watching the young ravens' awkward first attempts at flight was amusing,
although there is nothing quite as annoying as the squawking of three
hungry raven chicks at 4 AM before first light on a June morning.

WOMEN OF THE LIGHTHOUSE, HOMES ON A ROCK, AND RECIPES

Women never served as light keepers at Split Rock, but they played a largely overlooked and underappreciated role in the history of the beacon. During the light's fifty-eight years of service, most of the thirty-five keepers were married, and their families lived with them atop the cliff while they kept the light shining. Following rigid gender roles, women carried out the work that raised children and kept families together.

During our years at the lighthouse, we had the wonderful opportunity to visit with many of the grown children of the keepers who had served at Split Rock decades earlier. They told us that life was lonely at times—so isolated at a lighthouse with only the two other keepers' families for company. We knew how that felt. Many of their reminiscences and some of their fondest childhood memories were of their mothers, the unsung women who nurtured them and made their families' houses homes.

A huge part of their work was feeding the family. Although so much has changed since the early years at Split Rock Lighthouse, one challenge has remained constant: stocking a pantry and cooking out of it when resupplies are infrequent. Early keepers' wives had to be expert planners. They waited for the supply boat to provide their groceries and staples such as flour, sugar, and canned goods. If they ran out of something, it meant a ten-mile round trip in the light station skiff to Mattson's general store in Beaver Bay. Fish, venison, moose, grouse, and berries were available from the lake and nearby forest. The women grew other staples such as potatoes, turnips,

Keeper Adam Sayles reclines on the front porch while his children play with the Covell children, about 1926.

and cabbage in the thin soil near the lighthouse. They cooked and baked with woodstoves, hand-washed clothes with lake water, mended clothing, sewed curtains, planted flowers and gardens, all while raising children on a cliff edge.

Although I was a historic site manager, not a light keeper, my family's life at Split Rock wasn't much different a century later. We were all lucky Jane could stay home when the children were young. We had the good fortune of electricity and running water. But I have always been a lousy cook. Jane is an excellent cook who prefers her pantry stuffed. She still needed to plan carefully, and she couldn't borrow from other keepers' wives. It was a hundred-mile, day-long round trip to Duluth for any major grocery shopping. We lived through enough blizzards, electrical storms, and power outages to learn the importance of always keeping a well-stocked pantry, root cellar, and freezer.

Jane's talents went beyond her cooking and baking and feeding our family. I still marvel at her resilience. She showed it in November 1985, when I was off hunting ducks and she and John, then an infant—both down with the flu—faced a gale blowing off the lake with seventy-mile-per-hour gusts. She had to deadbolt the door to keep it closed. For many years, Jane worked at the health clinic in Silver Bay, but she still found time to quilt, sew, chase bears and deer from her garden, tend our cuts and bruises, and plant and tend all of the flowers around the lighthouse grounds—all while guiding and nurturing our children to grow into solid, caring adults. Simply put, she made our house a home. Thanks to Jane, we lived our best life at Split Rock. I am deeply grateful for her loving partnership in a most eventful life.

In a continuing demonstration of our partnership, I've persuaded Jane to share some of her recipes and stories, in her own words.

Jane and the kids, 1987

Jane's flowers on our front porch, 2017. The rose bush in the foreground was planted by Edith Covell in the 1930s.

SOUR CREAM RHUBARB CAKE

I loved my rhubarb patch in the corner of my garden behind the storage barn. I actually imported a plant with me from southern Minnesota that produced the big stalks and leaves I remembered from childhood. I had another plant that produced smaller stalks with beautiful red interiors.

1 ½ cups sugar
½ cup melted butter
1 egg
1 cup sour cream

1 teaspoon vanilla
1 teaspoon baking soda
2 cups flour
1 ½ cups chopped rhubarb

TOPPING:
⅓ cup sugar
1 teaspoon cinnamon

Grease a 9×13 pan and set aside. In a mixing bowl combine sugar, butter, egg, sour cream, and vanilla. Mix well. Stir in baking soda and flour. Add rhubarb and mix to combine. Spread batter in pan. In small bowl combine the sugar and cinnamon. Sprinkle over batter and bake at 350 degrees for 30–35 minutes.

~~~

OVERNIGHT CRABAPPLE JUICE

The crabapple tree in our backyard between the two storage barns provided a good perch for the kids to climb. They'd toss down the little ripe crabapples for the dog to eat, enjoy—and puke up later in the house. Neither the kids nor the dog was ever sufficiently contrite.

I could stand on a ladder to reach and pick enough crabapples to make juice to last all winter. I left the crabapples higher up and out of reach for the bears, cedar waxwings, and grouse to devour.

4 quarts crabapples
5 quarts water
2 teaspoons cream
   of tartar
2 cups sugar

Remove stems and cut crabapples into quarters—do not core or peel (like anyone would want to do that). Bring water to a boil and dissolve cream of tartar in water. Pour over crabapple pieces and let sit overnight. In the morning, drain liquid through several layers of cheesecloth (I rarely had cheesecloth so I just ran it through a strainer and called it good). Add sugar to offset sourness. It makes a beautiful pink tart juice. Freeze in small containers. At Christmastime, a crabapple cocktail of vodka, crabapple juice, and Sprite is more than quenching.

~~~

ROASTED GROUSE IN WINE SAUCE

Hunted ruffed grouse, also known as partridge, is a North Shore tradition every autumn. With the dog as a companion, Lee would often come home with a bird or two in his hunting vest. After he cleaned the birds, I would rinse and examine the grouse breasts for shotgun pellets and bite marks. Our retriever was a marginally trained hunting partner, but he dearly loved to hunt, so Lee had to race to get to the downed bird before the dog did.

    8 slices bacon
    4 boneless grouse breast halves
    1 cup chicken broth
    1 cup white wine
    2 onions, chopped
    4 cloves garlic, chopped
    salt and pepper

Fry bacon slightly, not until crisp. Remove and set aside. Brown grouse breasts in the same pan quickly, about two minutes per side. Remove grouse pieces and wrap each with two slices of bacon. Secure with toothpicks. Place grouse pieces in baking dish along with broth, wine, onion, garlic, salt, and pepper. Roast uncovered at 325 degrees for about 45 minutes.

~~~

WILD RICE SALAD

Even if you, like me, are not a huge fan of wild rice, this salad makes a perfect partner on the plate with roasted grouse.

  1 cup wild rice
  4 cups chicken broth
  juice of 1 lemon
  1 cup diced red bell pepper
  1 cup diced yellow bell pepper
  1 cup diced celery
  ½ cup sliced scallions
  1 cup chopped toasted pecans

VINAIGRETTE:
½ cup rice wine vinegar
½ teaspoon sugar
1 tablespoon low-sodium soy sauce
2 teaspoons minced garlic
¼ teaspoon ground ginger
½ cup olive oil
salt and pepper

Cook wild rice in chicken broth until rice grains split open and rice is tender. Drain the rice and squeeze lemon juice over it and set aside to cool. Whisk together vinaigrette and pour over cooled rice. Add red and yellow bell peppers, celery, and scallions and stir them in. Toss in toasted pecans.

〜〜

Meat Marinade

I was shopping for groceries at Zup's in Silver Bay one day. Walking by the meat counter, I was surprised to see three enormous moose roasts. They were so big each one would have easily fed a dozen people. Having never prepared a moose roast, I had to give it a try. It tasted incredible and we had leftovers for days. This marinade also works well for venison; the recipe makes enough for a 3- to 4-pound roast. Cook roast according to preference.

1 ½ cups salad oil
¾ cup soy sauce
¼ cup Worcestershire sauce
2 tablespoons dry mustard
2 ½ teaspoons salt
1 tablespoon pepper
½ cup wine vinegar
1 ½ teaspoons dried parsley
⅓ cup lemon juice
2 cloves garlic, crushed

Mix marinade ingredients together. Use to cover meat for 24 hours.

~~~

BLUEBERRY COFFEECAKE MUFFINS

Picking wild blueberries and raspberries is a passion on the North Shore, and most everyone has their secret patch. I am not sharing mine. Berries are best eaten as you pick them but when disciplined enough to save some, I laced them into muffins or scones.

    ¾ cup butter
    1 ½ cups sugar
    3 large eggs
    1 ½ teaspoons vanilla
    1 cup sour cream
    ¼ cup milk
    2 ½ cups flour
    2 teaspoons baking powder
    ½ teaspoon baking soda
    ½ teaspoon salt
    1 pint fresh berries

Cream butter and sugar. Add eggs, vanilla, sour cream, and milk. In separate bowl, sift together flour, baking powder, baking soda, and salt. Add flour mixture to batter until just mixed. Fold in berries. Bake in muffin pans at 350 degrees for about 25–30 minutes.

GROWING UP at the lighthouse, John and Anna always lived with dogs and cats as pets. Our first dog, Ozzie, arrived the week I was hired at Split Rock in 1982. In our first few months of living at the lighthouse, Jane and I decided that a cat would fit in. So we stopped at the animal shelter in Two Harbors and picked out a little black and white kitten to take home. Since we had Ozzie the dog, we named the cat Harriet. Months later, we changed Harriet's name to Harry for obvious reasons.

We'd grown so smitten with our golden retriever, Ozzie, that after our first year we decided we could handle two dogs at the lighthouse. One of the Split Rock tour guides was moving away and couldn't take Dolly, who was also a golden retriever. Jane had fallen in love with Dolly when she first met the dog, so the owner knew we would take good care of her. He failed to inform us that she might be pregnant until about a week after he dropped her off—just as we learned that Jane was pregnant with John.

Anna reads to Captain, 1991.

Captain joins the kids in the trailer, 1992.

Dolly gave birth to ten puppies in late February in the basement of our house. Suddenly, we were living with twelve golden retrievers, and cleaning up after those puppies fell to me. By May, things were getting hectic, with a new baby coming, ten rambunctious puppies, and the lighthouse opening for my second summer season as site manager. Jane and I managed to get all those squirming little puppies down to the Lake County Veterinary Clinic in Larsmont, where they were inspected and given shots. But as cute and fun as puppies can be, they became too much for us to handle. We needed to figure out a way to find new homes for them.

It turns out, selling the puppies was easy. They were purebred golden retrievers and about as cute as puppies come. One warm day, we took them out in the yard so they could play. Visitors walking to the lighthouse saw those furry puppies and just gravitated over to the fence to visit with us and pet them. Before we knew it, someone asked if they were for sale.

Dolly and Ozzie, with Jane and kids, 1989

Puppies, spring 1984

We knew the father of the puppies was also a golden retriever, but since we lacked any official papers, we didn't charge much—just enough to cover our investment in vet care and shots. Within a week, we sold them all. One couple purchased one of the pups and left—only to return a half hour later, asking for a second one. Dolly was a sweet old girl, and she lived many happy years with us at the lighthouse.

Anyone who knows dog breeds knows that golden retrievers are gentle and caring around children. Our young children always had a dog or two trailing along as they explored their world around the lighthouse. Three golden retrievers were followed by Shamus, a yellow Labrador retriever. We all learned to love and grow with the dogs.

Along with the happy times, adopting animals meant enduring the agony of losing longtime companions that had become part of the family. We all shared in the sadness when four lighthouse dogs and two cats died during our years at Split Rock. We gathered as a family, burying them in out-of-the-way places in the woods near the lighthouse. They all enjoyed idyllic lives.

~~~

GARAGE SALE

One September, I talked Jane into having a garage sale in one of the storage barns that we used as a garage. What was I thinking? Get rid of some stuff, lots of traffic already here and walking by—okay, let's do it. It was the usual work associated with holding a garage sale: haul your sellable items out, price it all, and sit there all day while shoppers offer you ten cents on the dollar for your old valuables. We thought we had a great clientele as all the visitors to the lighthouse would walk right past the gate to our yard. Put up a sign and we would sell all of our old stuff. Well, they came, and they looked. Trouble was they thought we were part of the lighthouse tour, and they began peeking in the windows of our house. When they started taking photos of our house and the lighthouse from our front yard, we figured it might be less intrusive just to haul our old stuff down to the Goodwill store in Duluth, which we did. That was our one and only time holding a garage sale at Split Rock.

THE WORD "SMELTING" can describe the process of applying heat to an ore to extract a base metal. But smelting means something different come April along Minnesota's North Shore. That's the time for smelt fishing—a unique practice, unlike the techniques used to hook most fish in the land of ten thousand lakes. All you need is a fishing license, a pair of hip boots, a dip net, and a bucket ... or a big cooler. There's no limit to the number of smelt you can legally catch. Smelt were not native to Lake Superior but began showing up in the lake in large numbers in the 1950s. The heyday for smelt netting ran from the 1960s through the early 1980s, our first years at Split Rock.

Smelt enter the streams in vast numbers in late April as the water temperature warms. When the runs peaked in the 1960s, you could stand in water up to your knees and feel hundreds of them bumping into your legs as they swam upstream. Smelt are sensitive to light, so they swim into the mouths of the rivers after dark. That's when the netting, and the partying, begins. We drove down to the mouth of the Split Rock River after dark on cool May evenings. The beach filled with people standing around bonfires or lit lanterns—drinking beer or wading in the river to dip their nets before emptying them into five-gallon pails on the shore. The smelt run lasted for only a week or two, but many people watched their calendars to be at the river mouths for the fun.

The Beaver Bay smelt fry, historically held in the basement of the Green Door bar for a few weekends each May, became the highlight of the spring social season along the North Shore. The smelt fry was an annual fundraiser for the Beaver Bay Volunteer Fire Department. The women who organized and served, the Fire-ettes, earned a well-deserved reputation for preparing and serving this local delicacy. North Shore residents and smelters eagerly anticipated this feast and made a beeline to Beaver Bay to dig in. On weekends, a line of people waiting for a table snaked up the stairs from the basement and out into the Green Door's parking lot. The basement meeting room became a dining room for the fry, with folding tables and chairs to seat seventy diners at a time. As a table cleared and people left, you paid five bucks to be served a plate of smelt, coleslaw, a roll, and a carton of milk or, more likely, a cold beer from the bar upstairs. This was an all-you-can-eat affair, and the servers would refill your plate with the small, deep-fried fish for as long as you could eat them. Some of the prideful guys tried to see how many smelt they could eat. Smelt are small, sardine-like fish, about five inches long. Eating fifty at one seating was not unheard of.

What made the Beaver Bay smelt dinners so delicious was the way the fish were prepared. First, they were cleaned and beheaded. They were then "butterflied," the two meaty halves spread open. Then came the involved process of rinsing, seasoning, battering, breading, deep-frying, and a couple other secret steps that only the Fire-ettes knew and closely guarded. Smelt are so small that you eat the whole fish, bones and all. In the early 1990s, I began volunteering at the smelt fry each year—helping with smelt cleaning and cooking. It was a great way to reconnect with neighbors in town after a long winter, and maybe end the day with a free meal of smelt.

Our friends and relatives often came to stay with us when winter finally broke, around the time of the smelt run, and I would treat them to a meal at the smelt fry. To much local disappointment, the Beaver Bay Fire Department quit holding the spring smelt fry in the 1990s. The smelt runs in the North Shore streams had diminished, and there were not as many netters coming to the local streams to net smelt and attend the smelt fry. The reasons are a lesson in ecological balance. The major predators of smelt are lake trout. When the sea lamprey invaded Lake Superior in the late 1930s, they attacked the lake trout. Between commercial fishing and lamprey predation, the trout population collapsed—and the smelt population soared. But scientists found a way to kill off the lampreys, and they also stocked trout and salmon. Trout and salmon returned to higher numbers, and smelt numbers fell. People still net smelt at the mouths of many North Shore rivers, but the crowds and carnival atmosphere have largely disappeared. And there are still smelt fries held at various churches, VFWs, American Legion halls, and other places throughout Minnesota and Wisconsin. I have been to one or two, but none were as memorable as the May gatherings in the basement of the Green Door in Beaver Bay.

4.
≋ *Summer* ≋

I once asked Jane how she knew when summer finally arrived. "When the lilac bushes bloom in the yard," she answered. That would usually be the last week in June, but lilacs cannot be trusted.

Summer on the North Shore proves fickle and reluctant. June is mostly a month of fog and wind coming off Lake Superior. Often a June day starts with the sun warming the air and a gentle breeze coming down off the ridges. By midmorning, as the sun warms the land, the air rises to pull the colder air that had settled over the chilly water of the lake. That prompts the wind to change direction, and a cool lake breeze develops. A few weeks before, ice chunks floated on that water. The wind off the lake sometimes brings fog, and the fog can drop the air temperature from sixty degrees to the thirties in five minutes. You feel the cold mist on your face. I took to calling this an earache wind, and a stocking cap offered a good defense. Fog obscures the view of the lake, the shoreline, and even the lighthouse.

Jane didn't even bother to start planting flowers around the site until the middle of June. The plants took this cool June weather as an insult and refused to grow if planted any earlier. The cool, foggy, and windy weather of June often lasts until the Fourth of July. July visitors to the lighthouse are usually coming from points south and far from the lake-shore. They often dress in shorts, T-shirts, and flip-flops. By the time they walk from their cars to the gift shop in the visitor center, they're ready to purchase a sweatshirt or even a polar fleece jacket. We were more than happy to provide them cool-weather, Split Rock clothing.

By the second week in July, the weather usually settles down, and there is no place more glorious than the North Shore during the month or so of summer spanning July into August. Then—all too soon—the cool days and chilly nights return. July, August, and September are always the busiest times at the lighthouse, with the largest tour groups. On summer mornings the parking lot would be half full of cars and twenty or thirty people could be waiting for us to open the doors of the visitor center at 10 AM. Running the site felt like riding rapids in a canoe—all you can do is push off the rocks. On the peak fall color weekends there would be as many as four thousand visitors at the site. The goal for the staff was to make every visitor's question seem like it was the first time the guide had heard it. Lines formed as people waited to climb the stairs in the lighthouse. On the very busy days, we had to station a guide at the bottom of the spiral staircase and one in the lens room at the top and allow twenty-five people up at a time. Each guide would give up to five twenty-minute tours each day. On windy days, when they had to shout to be heard, they were often hoarse by day's end.

A busy Sunday on Labor Day weekend, 2013

INSPECTIONS

Sometimes on a schedule but often by surprise, inspectors from light-house district headquarters regularly stopped at Split Rock. They loved nothing more than sneaking up on the light station to surprise the keepers.

They came from the east after inspecting Apostle Islands lighthouses, making early-morning approaches to Split Rock. That made the lighthouse tender boat harder for keepers to see in the rising sun reflecting off the lake, according to Clarence Young, son of Split Rock's first head keeper, Orren "Pete" Young.

Light keepers prided themselves on not being caught off guard by these surprise inspections. The keepers even recruited the children at the lighthouse as an early warning system. Clarence Young recalled standing for hours with the other children, on the observation deck near the base of the lighthouse, watching to see who spotted the boat first. The first kid to see the lighthouse tender approaching in the morning glare could warn the keepers and win a reward of fifty cents. While the inspector anchored offshore and rowed to Split Rock, the head keeper could don his uniform and run down the stairs to meet the inspector at the dock.

The annual inspections looked at all aspects of the light station operations, right down to the light keepers' efficiency. The inspector examined all the buildings, including the homes of the keepers' families. The daughters of keeper

The lighthouse tender *Amaranth,* 1929

Franklin Covell, Beulah and Ileana, remembered one inspection of their house in the 1930s. They lived in the middle home at Split Rock, the same one we lived in. Their mother, Edith Covell, had taken it upon herself to stencil a decorative border near the ceiling on the walls in their kitchen—Lighthouse Service regulations be damned.

The inspector walked through the kitchen and the rest of the house. Just before leaving, he solemnly asked who was responsible for the border. Edith Covell, somewhat defiantly, said that she was. The girls thought: *uh-oh.* But the inspector smiled and said, "Well, I'm glad to see that someone around here has some imagina-

The lighthouse interior had to be spotless: cleaning room, hall-way, staircase.

tion." On another trip to Split Rock, an inspector caught Edith and the girls unprepared. They had just enough time to straighten the kitchen, hiding dirty dishes in the oven.

A typical inspection featured a walk around the grounds with the keeper, a review of supply inventory, and condition checks of the lighthouse and fog signal equipment. Inspectors would comb through the keeper's logbook to make sure it was up to date. If the light station passed muster, the inspector placed his signature in the keeper's logbook for that day.

Decades later, inspections still marked my years at Split Rock. Once a year, my bosses from the Minnesota Historical Society headed up from St. Paul to review my performance. Like the keepers from the early days, I found annual reviews a time for me to push for needed repairs, enhanced equipment, and additional staffing. In addition to the annual reviews, my supervisors visited during construction and preservation projects at the site, often meeting with contractors and architects.

Jane reminded me of one such visit in 1984 when she was nine months pregnant and my boss, John Ferguson, paid a visit during restoration work on the three keepers' dwellings. We were adding insulation in the attic and updating plumbing in our upstairs bathroom. Jane had just gone into labor and was resting on the couch in our living room. I gave her a heads-up that Ferguson and two of the contractors wanted to inspect the work. Not surprisingly, she was less than thrilled with me for parading these guys through our house. The men greeted Jane sheepishly. They felt even worse when they saw the five-gallon pail in the hallway—our toilet until the bathroom was finished. After inspecting the work upstairs, Ferguson beat a hasty retreat with apologies to Jane. He urged the contractor to hurry up and get the bathroom working again. The next day a healthy eight-pound, three-ounce baby boy, John Byron Radzak, arrived at the Two Harbors hospital.

Split Rock's isolated, cliff-top perch meant headquarters were always far away. From the US Lighthouse Service days (1910–39) when supervisors were in Detroit, to the Coast Guard era (1939–69) when bosses were based in Cleveland, to my years with oversight from St. Paul, management was never nearby. That meant keepers had to be self-sufficient and flexible, adapting to changing conditions, equipment failures, and unexpected moments. We all needed to act independently while taking responsibility for our actions. That independence and isolation combined to make the job desirable to the light keepers—and to me.

At least I didn't have to greet my supervisors wearing my keeper's uniform. *Bruce Roberts, 2012*

Summer celebrations, meanwhile, began popping up along the North Shore: Bay Days in Silver Bay and Beaver Bay, Heritage Days in Two Harbors, and the Fisherman's Picnic in Grand Marais. We enjoyed the parades and festivities when we were able to get away from the lighthouse. I often dreamed of entering a Split Rock float in local parades. But the summer staff at the lighthouse and I were too busy to build parade floats or ride in parades. The Kiddie and Pet Parade at Heritage Days in Two Harbors was a family favorite when our kids were young. Main Street was closed off to traffic and the little parade rolled right through town. John and Anna led Dolly, our gentle golden retriever. Local parents smiled through the tugged and tangled leashes as happy dogs greeted each other and sniffed fire hydrants along the parade route. We also loved the talented Two Harbors City Band's summer concerts on Thursday evenings in the Thomas Owens Park band shell.

~~~

DURING THE SUMMER OF 2011, a statewide government shutdown brought unprecedented changes to the site. The infamous shutdown was ludicrous and untimely. The Democratic-Farmer-Labor governor and the Republican-controlled state legislature failed to agree on a spending bill by the July 1 start of the 2011 fiscal year. That meant all state services were shut down and all "nonessential" state employees were furloughed. That included state license bureaus, state offices, state parks, and state historic sites. At the busy start of the tourist season, Fourth of July weekend, no one could buy a fishing license. There were neither services nor staff at state parks across Minnesota. At Split Rock, I was forced to lay off all thirty-five historic site staff members until the legislative stalemate was settled. As site manager, I was deemed essential for the security of the site, and I continued to work.

The Minnesota Department of Natural Resources announced that all state parks would be completely closed to the public. That sparked an immediate public outcry, and the DNR backpedaled. Even though there were no staff in the parks—and no garbage service, no toilet paper, no emergency services—the public could walk into the state parks while leaving their vehicles at barricaded park entrances.

To add to the shutdown tumult, the five-mile-long section of Highway 61 through the state park was undergoing total reconstruction that summer. When the shutdown hit, construction was at the critical point of new alignment, but no asphalt had been put down. Since this was a state project, the highway construction came to a standstill on July 1. Contractors were told to go home until the shutdown was over. With heavy summertime traffic on the highway and no flaggers or transportation department employees on the job, traffic descended into chaos as potholes, dust, and mud grew. Adding to that mess, all day long visitors parked their cars and campers haphazardly along the construction zone outside the barricaded park entrance.

As the resident historic site manager at Split Rock, my shutdown orders came from the Minnesota Historical Society in St. Paul: close all gates and bar public entrance to the historic site. Considering the lack of staff, this made sense for the protection and safety of the visitors, as well as the historic lighthouse, the visitor center, and the three keepers' dwellings. All twenty-six Minnesota state historic sites were shuttered for the duration of the shutdown. On the evening of June 30, DNR state park staffers put up barricades at the park entrance at Highway 61, which also served as the entrance to the historic site. With barricades up until the

Summer shutdown at the park entrance, July 2011

shutdown ended, Jane and I were the only people left in the state park and at the lighthouse—a very strange feeling. (John and Anna had moved away by then.) For us, this had always been such a busy time of year.

After a wet and chilly June, that first day of July—Day One of the 2011 shutdown—dawned warm and sunny. It was the start of another beautiful Fourth of July weekend. Jane and I quickly caught a glimpse of a new reality that would last for twenty-one days. By 10 AM that first morning, visitors started to park at the highway and hike the half mile up the hill to see the lighthouse. Young parents with kids in strollers, old folks in wheelchairs, people carrying coolers, people with dogs on leashes—all had to be stopped at the gate and told that the historic site was closed. I spent most of every day at the gate to the site, passing out maps that showed shoreline spots to photograph the lighthouse. But no one could visit the lighthouse itself.

Most Minnesotans were understanding, at least of the orders I had to enforce. None of us could completely comprehend the intransigence in St. Paul. Many tourists from other states and foreign countries were baffled at why Minnesota leaders were closing parks and historic sites at the height of the season. There were always some bad eggs, and some people

People who walked into the park found this barricade at the entrance to the historic site.

just plain ignored the rules and hopped fences and attempted to sneak up to the lighthouse on the cliff. Jane stationed herself in our yard near the lighthouse, quick to turn these violators around as politely as possible if they sneaked past me at the gate or walked to the lighthouse along the shore from the state park.

By 2011, Jane and I had been living at the lighthouse for nearly three decades. We never dreamed that the historic site would be closed at the outset of the busiest time of the year. But there was a bright side. It allowed us to experience the lighthouse in the summer the same way as the first light keepers, in the 1910s—before the North Shore highway opened up the beacon to hordes of tourists. During the three-week shutdown, we sat on our porch in the evenings and basked in the quiet serenity. We were the only people in the state park.

Visiting moose, 2011

We were amazed just how quickly wild animals returned once the tourists left. Ravens and falcons swooped lower. Deer, woodchucks, and snowshoe hare fed on the grass in the yard near the lighthouse. On Day Four, a cow moose trotted up out of the ravine along the park road while I visited with people at the park entrance. There was still plenty of foot traffic on the park road, with people hiking in and out of the park. The moose nearly bowled over a couple and headed up the hill and into the park. Early in the morning of Day Eleven, as I wolfed down a quick breakfast, Jane looked out the stairway window toward the lighthouse. Then she whispered, "Get the camera and, whatever you do, don't let the dog out!" The moose stood at the chain-link fence, making a breakfast of the Virginia creeper vines climbing the fence twenty feet from the front porch—up close and personal. I managed to shoot a couple of quick photos before she ambled down the path to the visitor center. We saw her once more, on Day Seventeen, when she returned for another breakfast of Virginia creeper.

That summer of 2011 marked the only time in our thirty-six years at Split Rock that we closed the historic site to the public. In my report, I estimated that we turned away an average of 906 daily visitors—or more than nineteen thousand, all told. Despite the stress of personally turning these people away, Jane and I appreciated the feeling of timelessness the shutdown brought to our corner of Lake Superior. We felt a hint of the lives of those early keepers' families—isolated on the rock for the summer.

～～

PARK AND SITE, BUILDING TRAILS AND COMMUNITY

When I was a kid, my family used to stop at Split Rock Trading Post on camping trips to the North Shore. I remember the sadness I felt seeing the black bear cubs that the shop owner had locked in a large cage. I also recall seeing the huge anchor from the *Madeira* on display near the trading post. And that anchor tells a tale that ties the boat to the lighthouse, to the park, and to avid scuba divers.

The *Madeira* was a schooner-barge—a vessel built to carry maximum cargo and use its sails to aid the steamer that towed it. In the famous storm of November 1905, as the steamer *Edenborn* was towing the *Madeira* across the lake, the steamer's captain realized that both vessels were in trouble and cut the tow line. The *Madeira* smashed into the Gold Rock cliffs, where huge waves pounded

the wreck. Facing death, sailor Fred Benson timed his leap from the ship to the shore and scrambled up the cliff with a rope. Benson was able to save eight of the nine crew members. The wreckage came to rest just offshore in water depths between thirty and one hundred feet. Split Rock Lighthouse was built, in part, because of that wreck.

While the bottom of the massive lake holds more than three hundred shipwrecks, including many in Minnesota waters, most are either too deep or too far from shore for recreational scuba divers. In the 1990s, some Minnesota scuba clubs and the Great Lakes Shipwreck Preservation Society floated the idea of deliberately sinking an old iron ore carrier off the shoreline of Split Rock Lighthouse State Park as a recreational diving at-

traction. The state considered the idea, and I was thrilled to board the Coast Guard buoy tender *Sundew* and ride along as the cutter sailed back and forth just offshore from Gold Rock Point and Split Rock, surveying possible sites. I relished the chance to talk with the fifty-five crew members and snap some photographs from the unique vantage point of a large ship deck.

At the same time, the *Madeira* had become a wildly popular dive site for cold-water scuba divers. It's a short swim to the wreck from a beautiful pebble beach. In 1992, the *Madeira* was placed on the National Register of Historic Places. After lengthy review, the idea of sinking a ship was nixed. Decision makers thought it would jeopardize the historic wreck site and compromise the authenticity of Split Rock Lighthouse. The DNR built a parking lot, a vault toilet, and a short trail for access to the *Madeira*.

In the early 1990s, the owners of Gold Rock Point posted a "For Sale" sign near the highway, where the footpath to the point started. Both the state park and the site staff feared that a developer might purchase the point and build condominiums—ruining the pristine view from the lighthouse and the historic nature of the *Madeira* shipwreck site. In 1997, the Minnesota Parks and Trails Council helped the state park add an eighty-one-acre parcel of land that included Gold Rock Point. In 2010, the DNR purchased the nineteen-acre parcel across the highway from Gold Rock Point and added it to the state park.

The *Madeira*'s anchor, salvaged from the wreckage in the 1970s by a diving club, was displayed at the Split Rock Trading Post until it burned down in 1999; that area along Highway 61 became part of an important parcel added to the state park in 2010. And thanks to the generosity of the owners, the anchor was donated to the Great Lakes Shipwreck Preservation Society. Through their dedicated efforts, the anchor was loaned to the Minnesota Historical Society and displayed at the entrance to the Split Rock Lighthouse Visitor Center.

That was just one of the many improvements made to the state park over the years, and I loved working with the DNR on those enhancements. Perhaps my favorite project started in the late 1980s, when we aligned the new Superior Hiking Trail.

A small group of hiking enthusiasts realized the beauty and exceptional vistas from the highest ridges that parallel the shoreline of Lake Superior. They formed the Superior Hiking Trail Association in 1986 and began working with the DNR to develop a 150-mile walking path from Duluth to the Canadian border. Tom Peterson, who worked for the Minnesota DNR, hiked the hills and valleys of the North Shore nearly solo to lay out the route of the new trail. By 1987, he was flagging its fourteen-mile path through the high country between Gooseberry Falls State Park and Beaver Bay, Minnesota. Since I knew this country so well, Tom graciously allowed me to make suggestions on his topographical maps—highlighting the most scenic routes and elevations along the ridges behind Split Rock. (This was before the days of GIS, GPS, and Google Maps.)

After it was built, I volunteered as the section leader and helped maintain the trail. It gave me a good excuse to hike the trail and enjoy the woods. The breath-stealing views give hikers awesome vantage points on Lake Superior, all the way to the Boundary Waters Canoe Area to the north.

The North Shore is really a 150-mile-long

Split Rock Lighthouse State Park encompasses over two thousand acres of heavily forested rocky uplands and almost four miles of continuous Lake Superior shoreline.

Congressman Jim Oberstar, an avid bicyclist, cuts the ribbon for the trail through Split Rock Lighthouse State Park, August 2002.

linear community, and I took great pleasure carving out my role in that world. In the late 1990s, I joined residents who called themselves the North Shore Touring Trail Association. They had started planning a paved bicycle trail. We wanted to create a kind of North Shore sidewalk, connecting the towns of Schroeder, Tofte, and Lutsen. By 1999, the DNR embraced the concept of a trail between Highway 61 and the lakeshore, extending it all the way from Two Harbors to Grand Marais, more than eighty miles up the shore. They renamed it the Gitchi-Gami State Trail.

Construction began near the towns of Schroeder and Tofte. I assisted in planning the trail segment through Split Rock State Park to Beaver Bay. I believed the bike trail would give visitors a new and fun way to access the lighthouse. We wanted to pave the trail as near to the shoreline as possible, especially within the state park. That meant some challenging grades and curves. But the section opened in 2003, and I took pride in serving on the board of directors, even as president of the Gitchi-Gami Trail Association until 2009.

The story of Split Rock's growth and development as a popular tourist spot is really one of years-long cooperation between the state park and the historic site. The two continued to work together as hosts each May for sixth-grade visitors and events such as Lake Superior Day, National Lighthouse Day, and the *Edmund Fitzgerald* beacon lighting. Some of our teamwork was less

apparent but equally vital. We joined forces on signage, maintenance, and plowing for entrance roads and trails—not to mention planting white pine seedlings to regrow the original pine forest that thrived along the North Shore more than a century ago. I enjoyed using my archaeological training and lending a hand to investigations of some of the historic sites within the state park, including the Split Rock Lumber Company logging camp at the mouth of the Split Rock River and the Little Two Harbors commercial fishing settlement. From the *Madeira* shipwreck to the realignment of Highway 61, the work was varied and fascinating. And efforts to make the park and historic site even more accessible for recreation are ongoing. A large vehicular campground on the upper side of Highway 61, straight back from the lighthouse, was scheduled to open late in 2021. And several tracks of the Split Rock Wilds, a large mountain biking trail system on Lake County land between the state park and Beaver Bay, were completed in 2020. The beauty of the North Shore just doesn't quit, and neither do the people who find new ways to enjoy it.

EACH SUMMER BROUGHT other wildlife sightings, of course. Every year a family of coyotes lived within a stone's throw of the main parking lot. We rarely saw them, but on many nights we heard them calling, and on many mornings I found a set of new tracks where they patrolled the lighthouse paths and trails. When an ambulance or highway patrol flew by on the highway with sirens wailing, we listened for the coyotes—the sirens are the perfect pitch to set them all answering. I often wondered what the campers in the state park thought when they heard this chorus responding.

Bear interactions were to be expected in state parks on Minnesota's North Shore. In the early 2000s, the bear population around Split Rock grew. Black bears found their easiest meals around people—in the garbage cans and dumpsters around the lighthouse. Night after night, bears woke me, knocking over garbage cans and scattering their contents. Each night I tried to chase them away, and each morning I cleaned up the mess. Finally, I'd had enough. We had to do something. I contacted the Minnesota DNR and asked if they would deliver a live trap to catch one particularly brazen bear during his nightly forays.

Live traps to snare bears are basically large steel culverts or tubes mounted on a trailer with a grill welded at the front end and a trapdoor at the back. To catch a bear, you raise the trapdoor with a rope that's attached to some bait inside the tube, usually garbage. When a bear enters the tube and grabs the food it releases the rope and the trapdoor falls like

A visiting bear kept a low profile in 2010.

a guillotine, trapping the bear inside, unharmed and ready for transport and release far from campgrounds, people, and garbage. The DNR delivered the trap to our site late one day and left it for me to bait and set.

About midnight, I heard the familiar refrain of a bear knocking over garbage cans, looking for supper. Darn. I hadn't yet baited the trap. I was so fed up with garbage spread all over the parking lots that I decided to set the trap immediately, to catch the bear by morning. We had baked a chicken for supper, so I gathered the picked-over remains of the bird for bait. Since it was a warm August night, I headed out in my bathrobe, carrying the bones in my hands. At the trap, with the chicken carcass in one hand and the rope for the trapdoor in the other, I heard a huffing and looked up. My headlamp illuminated the bear, standing on its hind legs directly on the other side of the trailer. His nose was in the wind, and our eyes met. He was smelling the chicken in my hand. Bears can be unpredictable. I knew the prudent thing to do was to get rid of the chicken in a hurry, so I pulled on the rope to raise the trapdoor and tossed the carcass deep into the trap. Slick as you please, as if he were trained to do it, the bear took a sniff and followed the bones as I dropped the door behind him. I could hear him crunching on the chicken bones, safely inside the trap. Snugging up my bathrobe with a sense of satisfaction and relief, I headed back to the house for a good night's sleep.

The next morning, when I went out to check on my trapped bear, I noticed that he had ear tags, which meant he had been trapped before. I soon learned that he was notorious. According to the DNR conservation officer who came to pick him up, he had been bothering campers on Stockton Island in the Apostle Islands National Lakeshore, straight across the lake and about thirty-five miles away from Split Rock, the summer before. The National Park Service had trapped him there, hauled him ninety miles south on the mainland, and released him in the wilds around Rice Lake, Wisconsin. Within a week, he had hightailed it back to Lake Superior and swum eight miles back out to Stockton Island. Park rangers named him "MacArthur" for his infamous long-distance return—a salute to US General Douglas MacArthur, who famously proclaimed, "I shall return" to free the Philippine Islands from Japanese occupation in World War II. Thankfully, we never again saw MacArthur the bear at Split Rock.

~~~

WE WERE EXCITED to have a pair of peregrine falcons nesting for several years along the cliff below the lighthouse. The crow-sized raptor can reach a dive speed, or hunting swoop, of two hundred miles per hour. I once watched from the lantern deck of the lighthouse as a peregrine folded its wings, dived, and hit a terrorized goldeneye duck as it lifted off the calm lake. The duck launched itself only about a foot or two off the water before the falcon hit it at full speed. It happened so quickly that all I could see was a puff of duck feathers and the falcon flying off with its meal. Reintroducing peregrines to Minnesota's North Shore of Lake Superior made for a wonderful success story. The fast-flying birds of prey had vanished from the Minnesota wild. But beginning in the early 2000s, the Minnesota Department of Natural Resources and the Midwest Peregrine Society established nesting locations on the high cliffs along the North Shore, such as Palisade Head, Gold Rock Point, and Split Rock, and at Northshore Mining near Silver Bay. They brought the peregrines back.

On the face of the 130-foot vertical cliff upon which the Split Rock Lighthouse stands, some seventy feet above the lake, a small shelf of rock jutted out about two feet. In 2009, I first noticed ravens flying to this ledge in February, carrying sticks to build a nest. For five years a pair of ravens used this cliff notch to raise families of squawking, noisy young. For some reason, they quit nesting on the cliff ledge, leaving it vacant for a season. A pair of peregrine falcons claimed the ledge the next year, taking up housekeeping and raising four fledglings. Three made it to adulthood.

The Midwest Peregrine Society returned in mid-June every year to band a new batch of young falcons. This helped the society and the DNR track the success rate of the nesting birds. Skilled climbers descended the cliff face on ropes. As the falcon parents protested loudly and made diving swoops, the climbers borrowed the young birds from the parents' nest for a few minutes—carefully lifting them up on a rope to the top of the cliff in a covered box. Up top, they quickly weighed, measured, extracted blood samples from, and banded the young. Holding the warm baby birds with oversized beaks and feet, even for only a few moments, really connected me to these amazing birds of prey. Each year they named the fledglings and, in 2016, they gave the Split Rock staff the opportunity to christen four fuzzy chicks. We named them Pete, Franklin, Beulah, and Grace after original light keepers and their children who lived on the rock in the early twentieth century.

Each year, the same falcons returned to raise a family on this cliff or others along the rugged North Shore. We watched every spring and through every storm to make sure they made it back.

~~~

Banding falcons, June 2017. For a surprise, check out the transport box at their feet.

IN OUR EARLY DAYS at Split Rock, I learned about the weather's unpredictability on the North Shore from Ragnvald and Ragnhild Sve and their son, Walter, whom we met at that Christmas party in our first year. They were members of a commercial fishing family, operators of Split Rock Cabins, and among our nearest neighbors.

In the 1930s young Walter Sve mended fishing nets at the knee of his father, and he spent most of his adult life fishing—a tradition he later passed down to his son, Eric. Walt had great respect for Lake Superior and the ferocity and suddenness of the storms it generated. In his Norwegian brogue, he told me how he hated the "dirty nor'westers," the name Walt and the other commercial fishermen gave to summer thunderstorms that developed fast. They roared from behind the hills of the North Shore to the west and rolled swiftly out over Lake Superior. If fishermen were out in their small skiffs tending the nets a mile or more from shore, they had no time to row to shore before the storms barreled out over the lake with lightning, thunder, hail, and high winds. The offshore winds made it nearly impossible in the old days to row back to shore before the storm struck. That left fishermen scrambling to tie their skiffs to their nets to keep from being blown across the lake. In 1935, Walt's father-in-law lost his life to hypothermia during one of these storms. He was tending his nets four miles out on the lake, and he couldn't get back to shore. Ten days later they found his frozen corpse in his skiff, washed up on the Wisconsin shore thirty miles from his nets. He apparently knew his fate and had tied himself to the boat so his body would be found.

A dirty nor'wester rolls in, August 2003.

I always respected and feared the lake and its quick-change nature. Even in the middle of the summer, the lake could never be completely trusted. That didn't stop us from paddling canoes for short jaunts near the lighthouse. But I kept a sailor's eye on the weather. And that isn't always easy. Once you launch a canoe or kayak on the lake, you're sitting right at lake level, where it's difficult to see the subtle warnings of impending wind or weather changes. We learned that lesson on a short family canoe paddle.

It was late July and the weather settled and calmed over Lake Superior. On a beautiful evening at the end of the month, Jane and I decided to take John and Anna for a short canoe ride along the shore below the lighthouse. It was a beautiful, placid day, and the lake was perfectly flat, without a ripple as far as we could see from the cliff top. There was no wind at all, and the sky was perfectly clear. We looked to the west. No thunderheads or threats of approaching summer storms. After a quick supper, the four of us grabbed life jackets and canoe paddles and I threw the canoe on my shoulders for the portage down the trail to the lake near the old tramway ruins. When we reached the shoreline near the small white pump house building, the lake was so flat that there wasn't even any gurgling or splashing among the rocks on the shoreline. The lake was like a mirror, its only motion a slow rise and fall of the surface that always happened when the lake was calm. It felt to me as if the lake had a rhythmic pulse and was breathing.

John and Anna were only about eight and six years old, but they were used to going on canoe trips with us. They sat in the bottom of the canoe while Jane paddled in the bow seat and I navigated from the stern. We made sure everyone was wearing their life vests as we launched the canoe out onto the flat surface of the lake. The air was warm, and the evening shadows from the trees along the shore fell out over the water. We planned to go out only a couple hundred feet from shore and to paddle near the base of the cliff below the lighthouse. The water was magical the first half hour. As we slowly paddled out from shore, we looked down into the crystal-clear water and saw every rock on the lake bottom. Near the base of the lighthouse cliff there were large boulders on the lake bottom about forty feet below, some the size of elephants. The water was so clear that on the dead-calm surface it felt to us like we were flying or floating in midair. Other than the occasional swirl of a paddle stroke or the wake of the canoe, the surface was an unbroken expanse reflecting the blue sky back at us.

Having already lived at the lighthouse for several years, both Jane and I were well aware of what the Duluth meteorologists called backdoor cold fronts. We'd seen them many times. They occur when a weather change far out on the lake causes an east wind to build and move like a freight train toward the North Shore. If you watch carefully, you will see these

John and me at the foot of the lighthouse cliff a couple of years after the backdoor cold front incident

A backdoor cold front blowing in from the lake, September 2014

fronts approaching. You won't notice a change in the weather on the shore or in the clear sky, but the water color changes to dark blue far out on the surface of the lake. Cold wind ripples the surface and approaches, sometimes at up to thirty miles per hour. When that ominous line hits shore, the east wind drops the air temperature as much as twenty degrees.

Out in our canoe, we had no clue that a backdoor cold front was brewing on the open lake on the other side of the lighthouse cliff. Luckily, we had stayed within a hundred feet of shore. I suddenly noticed the lake rippling off in the distance. The treetops on the cliff top near the lighthouse began to bend in the wind. We were near Ellingson Island and the Little Two Harbors Bay. There was no way to paddle back into the wind toward our launch site near the pump house at the base of the cliff. As the wind increased and waves grew, we paddled hard for the shelter of the bay, ran the bow of the canoe up onto the pebble beach, and climbed ashore. John and Anna thought the whole trip was a great adventure, but Jane and I breathed a huge sigh of relief. It was a close call. While Jane and the kids stayed on the beach with the canoe, I jogged the three-quarters of a mile back to the lighthouse and returned in our pickup truck. We strapped the canoe on the truck and headed back home in the much chillier evening. Later that night, in the warmth and safety of our house, we shared a wonder about those who came before. The Ojibwe and other Native Americans who lived around Lake Superior, and the French voyageurs who joined them, usually stayed close to shore as well. But somehow, they dared to venture out onto this lake in frail birchbark canoes. It simply astounded us that the people who had lived here for so many centuries had managed to steer birchbark canoes from the North Shore across about twenty miles of open lake to Isle Royale.

〜〜

PRESERVATION PROJECTS

By their very nature and purpose, lighthouses are built in some of the planet's most exposed places. From their remote perches, they face hurricane-force winds, freezing rain, and constant saltwater spray.

Great Lakes lighthouses, such as Split Rock, don't need to worry about salt but must endure constant freeze-and-thaw cycles. Because of the severe conditions, most Lake Superior lighthouses were built of stone, brick, or concrete. At Split Rock, a steel-beamed internal skeleton is sheathed with brick and concrete, while a cast-iron lantern on top protects its precious Fresnel lens.

Split Rock Lighthouse wrestled with fifty-eight Minnesota winters between its creation in 1910 and its retirement as a navigational aid in 1969. The US Lighthouse Service and then the Coast Guard made sure the light and fog signal operated effectively, but historic preservation was not on their radar. By the 1970s, it became clear that if we wanted to

Restoring the fog signal chimney and lighthouse, June 2009

maintain Split Rock as a showplace telling the story of lighthouses, we needed to rehabilitate it. Crumbling brick and concrete, peeling lead-based paint, and broken windows all cried out for repair.

As much as possible, the Minnesota Historical Society wanted to preserve the light station in its prime, early-1920s condition. That harkened back to the pre-highway era when the isolated lighthouse was accessible only by boat. There was no electricity to Split Rock back then. All water was either pumped up from the lake or collected from rainwater falling on the roofs of the keepers' dwellings and pooled in basement cisterns. The light keepers and their families rarely saw visitors in those early years.

Between 1982 and 2019, three major multi-year preservation projects punctuated my tenure at Split Rock—along with a multitude of smaller rehab jobs. Undertaking projects to improve access to the site and restore its aging structures became an annual rite. Some of these projects were obvious to the large groups of lighthouse visitors. In 1994, we built a wooden stairway to the lake and restored the tram house. In 1986, we constructed the eleven-thousand-square-foot visitor center and installed parking lot lights so we could

safely hold evening events such as the annual *Edmund Fitzgerald* memorial ceremony. Other projects went mostly unnoticed but were just as important. Asbestos and lead-paint abatement, for example, took time and money with little fanfare—as did burying a sewer line from the keepers' dwellings to the new septic system for the visitor center.

We dug into two other initiatives—no shovels required. In 2011, Split Rock secured a spot on the prestigious federal list of National Historic Landmarks. That honor cemented our national historical significance and made our site only the second such recognized lighthouse on the Great Lakes, after the Grosse Point Lighthouse on Lake Michigan.

Less glamorous but equally important, our 2016 cultural landscape report became a guiding document for planning at the historic Split Rock site. The report provides a comprehensive history of the site while recommending future enhancements from vegetation management to accessibility. All these efforts, from sewer lines to landmark nominations, put Split Rock on firm footing for future development and preservation on the site's twenty-five acres. It was a pleasure to take part in this work.

IN 2011, SPLIT ROCK SECURED A SPOT ON THE PRESTIGIOUS FEDERAL LIST OF NATIONAL HISTORIC LANDMARKS.

AS AN ANTHROPOLOGY MAJOR at St. Cloud State University in the 1970s, I read books by Carlos Castaneda, an American author who wrote about Mesoamerican shamanism. He introduced me to so-called places of power, or power spots, which I loosely interpreted to mean a place where a person feels a special connection with the earth and one's surroundings.

For our family, the lakeside porch of our home at Split Rock was that powerful place connecting us to our small corner of the earth. There was so much going on in that 180-degree view, facing straight south from the porch. The three keepers' houses all faced south, set about thirty feet

Our family on the front porch, 2018. From left: me, Anna, John, grandson Henderson, John's wife Hannah, and Jane.

back from the cliff, which is about a hundred feet up at that point. Sitting on the front porch, looking from left to right, we viewed the fog signal building and the lighthouse on their dome of anorthosite rock. Then our eyes gazed at the wide expanse of Lake Superior, all the way across to the Wisconsin shore twenty-five miles away. Farther to the right, the near shoreline in the state park came into focus, including Corundum Point, Little Two Harbors, and Day Hill. It was a panoramic view that never got old and never looked the same two days in a row.

Our porch received little use in winter but it was the go-to place to greet the sunrise with a cup of coffee or to relax at the end of the day in summer and autumn months. The only exceptions were calm muggy evenings when the mosquitoes drove us inside or the couple of weeks in July when the biting stable flies were relentless. It was our bridge to the natural world. On warm summer nights, we watched fireflies flash in their lazy flights across the yard. On a few special nights in August, we could see thousands of dragonflies erratically chasing mosquitoes at the cliff's edge in front of the house. We could watch the peregrine falcons train their young to swoop, dive, and hunt. In the spring we could sit on the porch while a doe and her fawns hungrily munched the newly sprouting grass in the nearby yard.

When our kids were young, the front porch was a safe haven and a won-

derful place to play in the warm sun. As they grew older, it became a place of learning, as Jane and I shared many conversations with them. We were fortunate to have occasional visits from past keepers—members of families who had served at Split Rock. Franklin Covell, a light keeper at Split Rock for twenty-three years, lived with his wife and children, in the center keeper's house, now our home, from the 1920s until 1944, when he retired as head light keeper. In the 1980s and 1990s, his daughters Beulah and Ileana visited us along with their husbands, who happened to be brothers: Mike and Otto Myers. We sat with Beulah on the front porch and spent a precious hour asking her many questions about her life in the same house. She told us about how her mother, Edith Covell, always had flower boxes full of colors on the sills of the porch. She pointed out the rose bushes near the front of the house that her mother first planted in the 1930s. They were still lush and full of red petals each summer. She told the story of how she and Ileana, the two keepers' daughters, met and married Mike and Otto, the two sons of a commercial fisherman from Beaver Bay.

Since most of our time on the front porch came in the warm summer weather, we had plenty of chances to watch storms, fog, rainbows, weird clouds, and lightning over the lake. It was always a changing landscape of half water and half sky, each reflecting and reacting to the other.

A panoramic view from our porch, 2017

In the early mornings and evenings, we had the light station more or less to ourselves. But while the lighthouse was open for tours, the grounds throbbed with bustle. Some summer days, two thousand people visited the lighthouse and grounds, with our home smack-dab in the middle of the action. Most of the visitors were considerate of our privacy when we were in our yard or on the porch. Sometimes, though, people would jump the fence or come in through the gates. We would find

Beulah Covell Myers visits with Jane and Anna, about 1990.

someone rummaging through our garage or even sitting on our front porch. We realized this was the high price we paid for living and working at a unique spot. Often that meant stepping outside our front door to find someone snapping a photo or petting our dog. Visiting with Beulah Covell, we learned that this tourist behavior was well entrenched. Back in the 1930s, her family also dealt with lighthouse visitors who would overstep their bounds. Social distancing was an unknown phrase back then. People peeked in their windows or even walked into their house. I found the small sign that Keeper Covell had painted when his superiors nixed his idea of building a fence. It read, "Please Respect the Privacy of the Keepers at This Station." I made another sign with the same message and placed it on the gate to our yard. Judging from how well the sign worked, there are a lot of illiterate people.

Those visitors who respected the chain-link fence around our yard asked many questions over the fence, usually when we were sitting on the porch or working or playing in the yard. The standard line of questioning went like this: "Do you live here?" "Do you live here year-round?" "Must be lonely." I wanted to say, *Well it would be, except for the fifty people walking by behind you*. But they seemed to be absorbed in the magic of another era, and that was a good thing.

～～

IT WAS ENDLESSLY FASCINATING to watch ships out on Lake Superior. The big lake's shipping season starts in late March when the Soo Locks open on the eastern end of Superior. And the story of shipping is, of course, deeply tied to the history and industrial development of the lake.

The Dakota called the lake Mdeyata, which means "at the lake." The Ojibwe called it Gitchigami, Big or Great Lake. The first French explorers renamed it Lac Superior, not only because it's by far the largest, but because it's also the first, or highest, of the five Great Lakes. It sits twenty-two feet or more above Lakes Huron, Michigan, and Erie, and 359 feet higher than Lake Ontario—the lowest and eastern-most lake. The steep drop-off comes thanks to Niagara Falls, which separates Lakes Erie and Ontario. In the 1950s, the St. Lawrence Seaway was completed, allowing ships to reach the Great Lakes from the Atlantic Ocean by way of the St. Lawrence River. Ships must wait in spring for the ice to melt on Lake Superior and the St. Mary's River, which connects Superior to Huron. Once the Soo Locks thaw, the big freighters can "lock up" the last leg of the journey into Lake Superior.

Before the Soo Locks were first built in 1855, all of the water leaving the lake flowed down rapids in the St. Mary's River and on into Lake Huron. The change came after the 1840s, with the large-scale development of copper mines. Native Americans had been mining copper around the lake for five thousand years, and the first European Americans to travel through had taken careful note. The lure of copper was a big part of the push for the United States to take the land from the Native nations who lived around the lake, including the North Shore. Through treaties signed in 1836, 1842, and 1854, the government forced the Odawa and Ojibwe to give up most of their lands in what are now Michigan, Wisconsin, and Minnesota, and to move onto small reservations around the lake. Prospectors located and claimed copper lands, and the government constructed locks to help transport that copper to the lower lakes. After the 1890s, the mining of iron ore on the iron ranges of northern Minnesota became a major part of this story.

During the past century and a half, as ships steadily grew larger and larger, the Soo Locks have been expanded several times. A ship enters the lock, the doors behind it are closed, and water is pumped into the lock until it lifts the ship to the water level of Lake Superior. Then the doors

It seems as if the cloud
show never stops.

at the front of the ship open, allowing easy passage at the level of the higher lake.

The main shipping lane cuts across Lake Superior about ten miles from Split Rock and Minnesota's North Shore. When the big lakers that load taconite along the North Shore are sailing in a direct route they pass much closer along the coast from loading points at Northshore Mining at Silver Bay/Two Harbors or to the twin ports of Duluth and Superior, Wisconsin. Many of these massive freighters stretch more than one thousand feet in length. They are nicknamed "lakers" because they work exclusively on the Great Lakes, mostly hauling taconite pellets. The little marble-sized chunks are a processed form of iron ore, extracted from open-pit mines in northern Minnesota and pelletized in nearby factories, then brought by rail to the lake. From there, the ships head down the lakes to giant smelting mills on the south shore of Lake Erie. Many people insist on calling these ships "boats" because they sail strictly on freshwater lakes. But I've been aboard some of these thousand-footers, marveling at their immensity and complexity, so I like to give them their due and call them ships.

The mammoth size of these thousand-foot iron ore carriers doesn't always protect them from Lake Superior storms. Two moments brought this home for me. I had a marine radio scanner in my office that allowed me to eavesdrop on some of the chatter between ship captains out on the lake. I didn't listen much, usually just during bad storms or when I saw some unusual ship traffic passing Split Rock. During a particularly bad November storm in the mid-2010s, I flipped on the scanner. It was raining, snowing, and blowing too hard for me to see more than a half mile out on the lake. The maritime weather station was broadcasting winds blowing out of the northeast at a steady thirty-five to forty knots (up to about forty-five miles per hour). Waves were swelling between twelve and eighteen feet. My scanner picked up a ship-to-ship channel, and I listened to the conversation between two captains on the lake. One captain asked the other how he was doing. The captain on the bridge of the other thousand-footer said he didn't care for the "dirty" weather. He wished he'd kept the ship in port and cringed at the notion of turning around out there. He feared turning sideways in the giant waves and troughs. This exchange told me that even these gigantic ships held great respect for Superior's storms.

Another time, I met the mother of a crewman who sailed on another of the big lakers. We began talking about ships, storms, and lighthouses. She told me that during a bad storm, her son called her on his cell phone from his ship, caught out on the lake. He calmly told her that it was pretty rough sailing out there, and their ship was getting thrown around some. He just wanted her to know that, whatever happened, he loved her very much. Her son later told her that his captain was worried enough about the ship going down in the storm that he told his crew they should call their loved ones if they could. Sailing on the Great Lakes, no matter the size of one's ship, still carries great danger.

~~~

A ship in heavy seas, 2008

WE LOVED FOGGY WEATHER, when the ships out on the lake sounded for fog on damp, misty nights. It was so soothing to lie in bed and hear the ships' foghorns bellowing from a dozen miles out on the lake. When two ships met in the night, and both were sounding for fog, it was as if they were sending each other mournful greetings. They unleashed a three-second-long blast every two minutes, enabling us to mark their passage in the dark as the signals faded away while they sailed toward Duluth or down the lake toward the Soo Locks.

I got to know the wheelsman who sailed on the *Edgar B. Speer,* one of the biggest ore carriers at 1,004 feet long and 105 feet wide. I asked him once if he thought he could see the Split Rock beacon when he sailed past. One pitch dark October night, he called me on my cell phone to say that the *Speer* would be passing Split Rock at about midnight. He would be on deck to watch for the beacon if I cared to light it up. Jane and I bundled up and walked up to the lighthouse. We could see the lights of the *Speer* coming up the lake from the Apostle Islands. I climbed the tower, wound up the weights to revolve the lens, and flipped the switch. My friend immediately called to say he could see the beam clearly. At one point, as we were talking, I stopped the rotation of the lens and aimed it right at the big ship. He said it was so bright, he could read a newspaper nine miles out on the lake.

I asked him if he would sound the foghorn on the ship, even though the night was crystal clear. He said he'd be willing to, although it might bother some of his sleeping crew. Still on the phone, he said, "Okay, here goes," and I could hear the horns sounding over the phone. From the shore, we listened. Nothing. We waited for nearly a minute before we heard the fog-horns, first faintly, then very loud and clear. We expected a delay, but that much time really brought home to Jane and me just how big the lake is, and how loudly those horns bellow. Before the wheelsman and I said good-night, I let him know that this marked the first time in fifty years—since its 1969 decommissioning—that the old Split Rock beacon had been lit specifically for a ship passing in the night. I never heard if his crew members were mad that he blasted a late-night foghorn. But he did say they loved seeing that old light shining for them from Split Rock.

〜〜〜

The *Edgar B. Speer* passes the observation deck on a bright day in December 2010.

The *Bounty*, a reconstruction of the 1787 British Royal Navy sailing ship, was built in 1960 for the movie *Mutiny on the Bounty*. It passed the lighthouse under motor in 2010.

BIG ORE SHIPS weren't the only ones floating around Lake Superior. After years of anticipation and hopeful rumors, Duluth officials invited vintage sailing ships to visit the port in August 2010—and every third year since—for the Tall Ships Festival (now Festival of Sail). Up to a dozen tall-masted schooners of various sizes sailed up through the Great Lakes, crossed Lake Superior, and spent a few days anchored in Duluth's harbor. Forty-five miles up the shore at Split Rock, we began watching a few days in advance to see their approach across the lake. That first year was so exciting. After all, sailing ships—large vessels with at least three square-rigged masts—had not been seen on Lake Superior in more than a century. They felt like part of a time warp as they sailed past Split Rock. There were few wooden sailing ships on the lake in 1909 and 1910, when the lighthouse was built.

Compared to the big modern steel ships, these schooners were small. But it was so impressive to see the sails unfurled as they tacked into the wind. During the few days that the ships docked in Duluth, thousands of people flocked to the port to watch them arrive. Many of the old boats offered tours. Several of the folks who came out to see the tall ships also visited Split Rock—receiving a special treat when these vessels from the past sailed near the lighthouse.

~~~

SOMETIME AROUND 2010, the centennial of Split Rock Lighthouse's construction, rock cairns began to appear on the shoreline below the lighthouse. At first, we found one or two of these carefully stacked piles of beach rock each day. Months later, it became a real fad among some park visitors who were serious rock stackers. We began hearing comments at the lighthouse from visitors who had seen the delicately balanced rocks along the shore. Some people, especially photographers, thought the cairns were an aesthetic annoyance, while others appreciated the artistic expression. The cairn makers believed the stacking was meditative.

People have been stacking rock cairns since prehistoric times, especially in the far north of Alaska, Arctic Canada, and Greenland. The Inuit people called them inuksuk, and they used them to mark places on the tundra, which has few natural landmarks. Hikers and travelers have long relied on rock stacks as trail markers. The twenty-first-century creative craze along the rock beaches of Minnesota's North Shore seems new—possibly driven by social media sites such as Facebook and Instagram. People build them and photograph them as a kind of message to say, "I was here and I'm leaving my mark." On my evening or early-morning patrols down to the

Rock cairns, 2010

shoreline, I was amazed to see dozens of rock stacks, some five feet high, piled up along the beach. They became a flashpoint. Some people loved them; others hated them. But everyone had to be impressed by the amount of time and effort that people were willing to put into building these stacks. Some of the rocks had to weigh well over one hundred pounds. With some of these piles balanced only a few feet from each other, I grew concerned about the safety of people walking around them. I'm not proud to say that I became a stack kicker. Every summer day, there would be new cairns built that needed to be toppled before the beach filled with people walking the shoreline. Maybe someday, I hope, people will go back to simply skipping stones out on the lake.

Rock painting, for lack of a more creative term, became another recent fad. People found smaller beach rocks, usually about the size of a hockey puck, painted them with bright, happy designs, and left them in odd places around the historic site. On the bottom side of the rock, they placed a sticker or painted their social media handle. Whoever found the rock would mark the discovery on social media. Our staff was picking them up all over the place, filling a box next to the recycling shed in the service area.

A couple of decades ago, geocaching became a big thing in state parks and other public areas. The DNR started a geocaching program, which it still operates. This appeared to be another hobby that spun out of social media and the internet. Someone hid a small plastic container in a hard-to-find, out-of-the-way place with a few small trinkets and a note. Then they posted hints about the hidden location on a geocache website. Other people tried to find it using global positioning system coordinates. We began finding these small containers hidden in strange locations around the historic site, such as under the roots of a tree, along a trail, or under the steps of one of the lighthouse buildings. At first, the containers baffled our staff. We didn't know what they were or what to do with them. We started finding the caches shortly after September 11, 2001—a time when everyone was jittery about suspicious items.

Like the cairns and the painted rocks, these geocaches are distractions for those visiting a beautiful historic place. We felt we had to remove them from the busy site, but many were left in more remote areas of the state park. Happy hunting.

~~~

FOR OUR LITTLE FAMILY, the most memorable times came when we had the lighthouse to ourselves. The historic site was open to the public every day, all year long, sunrise until sunset. When the last visitors left at dusk each day, the place was ours again. After dark, our nearest neighbors were the campers in the state park campground about a half mile away. We often saw their campfires glowing across Little Two Harbors Bay, but seldom heard anything besides the occasional barking dog.

August 27, 2008

Not that all nights were quiet. Far from it. My job required our living on site for a reason: to protect and secure an otherwise exposed and alluring location. People walked up to the lighthouse after dark at least three times a week, despite the closed gates and signs reminding them that the site shut down from sunset to sunrise. Some of these folks were just curious, but enough of them were up to no good—twisting doorknobs, trying to open windows, or just wanting to party.

The advent of digital photography made my job even more interesting. Drones equipped with video cameras were a real annoyance. They were not permitted at the site or in state parks, but people could launch them over us from a distance. Their irritating mosquito-buzz quickly became grating for us, especially when one was hovering in front of our bedroom window before dawn. They were a distraction for our tours—a drone might be flown at treetop height above twenty people who were trying to hear the guide. And as night photography grew easier, more photographers wanted to capture the lighthouse after dark.

I *always* kept an eye open and an ear tuned during all our years living at the lighthouse—even as I slept, ate, watched television, or played with the kids. When I heard sounds up near the lighthouse after dark, I threw on some clothes, grabbed a flashlight, and headed out to confront people with unknown intentions. I needed to stay alert not just after dark but any time after the rest of the lighthouse staff left for the day, when intruders thought there was no one around. Nothing got me out of bed faster than a phone call from the county sheriff saying a burglar or fire alarm had sounded at the Split Rock Lighthouse Visitor Center. Since the sheriff's office was at least twenty minutes away, I grabbed my flashlight, called the dog, and ran over to the visitor center to search for trouble before a deputy arrived.

One morning we were awakened at sunrise to the surreal shrieking of a man strutting back and forth near the lighthouse playing bagpipes. Sometimes, photographers shined powerful strobe lights on the lighthouse from the shoreline in the state park. I tried to ignore them and go back to sleep. I often saw photographers' headlamps and flashlights as they crept up the trail to get close shots of the lighthouse. It was my responsibility to enforce the rules, so I dressed, headed out, and asked them to leave. I was a lighthouse bouncer, in a way.

I found kids shooting off cherry bombs near the lighthouse after 3 AM. I had to stop people who were climbing up the outside of the lighthouse or rappelling down the cliff. Once during a restoration project, the lighthouse was surrounded by scaffolding. The workers cordoned off the ladders and platforms when they left for the day. That didn't stop people from breaking through the barriers and climbing the scaffolding to the top, and they had no interest in coming down. A few of these incidences

DECOMMISSIONING

It was a bad omen, back in the late 1950s. Reserve Mining built a taconite plant seven miles up the North Shore from Split Rock and installed a beacon, radio signal, and fog whistle at the entrance to the new harbor to guide ore carriers. These new navigational aids were cheaper than operating a fog signal and lighthouse. Light keepers weren't required. The Coast Guard and the Lake Carriers' Association agreed that a light at Split Rock was now redundant and unnecessary.

But Split Rock was still one of the nation's best known, most recognized lighthouses, as it had been in 1939 when the Coast Guard took over and noted that it was "probably the most photographed lighthouse in the United States." The Coast Guard, still recognizing the public relations value of a show-station lighthouse, operated it for a decade longer than needed to guide ships up and down western Lake Superior. To downsize, Split Rock's foghorn was taken out of service in 1961, and its staff was reduced to only two keepers. The station became mostly electrified and automated. Keepers merely performed a little maintenance and flipped a switch each night to turn on the thousand-watt lamp in the beacon before going to bed. And of course, they still greeted tourists in the summer.

In the early winter of 1968, the two keepers

59 YEARS

guiding ships up and down western Lake Superior

stationed at Split Rock shut down the beacon at the end of the shipping season as usual. But in January 1969, orders came down from Coast Guard District Headquarters in Cleveland: the light station was decommissioned, and they were to close it for good. The keepers boarded up the windows in their dwellings and left in February 1969. Coast Guard crew members stationed at Grand Marais were instructed to go to Split Rock and either pack up all of the equipment or haul it to the dump. It had always been customary for the Coast Guard to remove its Fresnel lenses from decommissioned lighthouses. In a move that flew in the face of that policy, the Coast Guard left the Fresnel lens assembly in place at Split Rock, and it became part of the property transferred to the State of Minnesota.

Split Rock Light Station's fifty-nine years as an aid to navigation had come to an end. The federal government classified Split Rock Light Station as surplus property, leaving the General Services Administration to dispose of the nearly eight-acre parcel. But the well-loved lighthouse was not done yet. Its next phase would grow with the development of Split Rock Lighthouse State Park. The beacon would continue to offer direction of a different kind. Split Rock's long tradition of luring tourist traffic was about to enjoy exponential growth.

became confrontational, but I was usually able to defuse the situation and rarely had to call for backup from the county sheriff.

Unfortunately, there were two suicides at Split Rock during our years there, which could neither be anticipated nor prevented. But accidents were minimal, and I felt proud of my security record. I helped visitors and staff stay safe. No Split Rock buildings were damaged during my watch. I spent many years longing for enhanced security measures, though. In 2016, the grounds and buildings were equipped with motion detectors, heat sensors, and security cameras.

~~~

A summer storm rolling out over the lake, July 2016

AUGUST WAS THE BEST time of year to spend late evenings out in the yard and up near the lighthouse. The lake warms up all summer, so clear nights stay balmy and we often sprawled out in the yard with the kids, usually between quilts. Some nights were so still and quiet that all we heard was the lake lapping on the rocks below or an occasional car passing on Highway 61 or the buzz of a few mosquitoes. We looked up at the stars and planets and shared stories with the kids, or just stayed quiet and soaked up the stillness. On some muggy nights, thunderstorms blew up from behind the ridges to the west. Huddling under the porch canopy, we followed the paths of the storms across the lake and watched the lightning move out across the water. We listened to the crack and rumble of thunder as the storm rolled over the Apostle Islands.

Lightning strikes were amazingly rare at Split Rock Lighthouse, despite the exposed, cliff-top buildings. They were all equipped with lightning rods. People think the rods attract any lightning that might strike in the area and conduct it into the ground, but that's not the case—they actually make buildings *less attractive* to lightning bolts. (There are some great YouTube videos on this.) It must have worked. We saw lightning strike tall spruce trees near the buildings and hit the lake several times, but we didn't see it strike the lighthouse. Once, a nearby hit knocked out our well pump and our phone system. After one particularly violent thunderstorm passed overhead, I walked up to the observation deck and stood near the lighthouse as the clouds passed. The rain was easing and the evening sun began to shine. I was puzzled by a loud and distinct buzzing sound coming from the top of the lighthouse. I could feel the hair on my arms standing on end. I assumed it had something to do with the passing storm and negative and positive electrical charges. The buzzing continued for several minutes and slowly dissipated. Just to be safe, I stayed away from the lighthouse that evening.

Thunderstorm, September 2015

〜

WE ALWAYS KNEW that our days living at Split Rock Lighthouse were numbered. As the years advanced more and more quickly, I looked ahead to retiring with equal parts trepidation and anticipation. For most people, retirement means you just quit doing a job or profession. For us, it would be a whole change in life and lifestyle. We would have to leave our home of thirty-six years, and at the same time I would end my job and pass on the responsibilities to someone new. As with all the light keepers that came before me, my job was my life, and my life was my job. I began my career at Split Rock when I was thirty years old and would be ending it when I was sixty-seven.

The one thing I knew for certain was that I wanted to retire in the spring. Spring would feel like we were leaving on a high note at the beginning of a new summer of opportunities and possibilities in our lives. We also wanted to be able to spend one last winter at the lighthouse, the time of year when we have our home and the site mostly to ourselves. That last winter the storms were more relished, the calm sunny days and clear quiet nights more savored. Leaving in April would also give me all winter to prepare the site and the staff and organize my office for a new site manager after one last busy summer. It also gave me time to resign from positions I held on committees and councils throughout the lighthouse and local communities, a time to say goodbye to the many colleagues and friends I had made.

During those last few years at Split Rock, Jane and I could also feel changes coming to Split Rock and the North Shore that made us realize it was time to move on. Traffic along the shore and at the site was unremittingly increasing each year, so much so that the site and the lighthouse were now open nearly year-round. In addition, an expansive new vehicle campground was due to be built in the state park in the next couple of years, which would bring ever increasing numbers of visitors to the site day and night. Drones and night photography were becoming more common as social media platforms for photos and videos of the lighthouse expanded. Besides, I was beginning to feel a little long in the tooth, and responding to nighttime security alarms and after-hours visitors felt more like work.

I was not really prepared for the interest shown in my retirement from Split Rock. Having one employer for forty-three years is rare nowadays, but I could not have been happier to work all those years for the Minnesota

Historical Society, first as an archaeologist and then at the lighthouse. The organization acknowledged my retirement with a press release that got the attention of statewide media and lighthouse museums throughout the country. The Split Rock staff caught me off guard with a surprise retirement party that touched me deeply. It was attended by many good friends from the North Shore community, and it was a bittersweet note to leave on.

On April 30, 2019, in a wet, sloppy snowstorm that covered the newly greening lawn, the moving van arrived, and the movers loaded our possessions aboard. After they drove away, we took one more walk through the empty house. Remembering all the happy years, Jane took a final photograph of the growth chart of the kids we had marked in pencil on the edge of the door in John's bedroom. Together in the quiet house with so many stories, we spent a few tearful moments etching into our memories the view of Lake Superior from our bedroom window. We both knew there was no need to, as it will always be with us.

The kids' growth chart records our years in the keeper's house.

Acknowledgments

WHEN I WAS FIRST HIRED by the Minnesota Historical Society in 1982 for the Split Rock job, I had no idea of the rich and varied life the position would lead to. From lighthouse museums around the country to personal connections along the North Shore from Duluth, Minnesota, to Thunder Bay, Ontario, I met many people who care deeply about their professions and communities. I worked with these folks for dozens of years, and to this day I remain close friends with many of them. I will always remember these relationships and what they have meant to me.

I wish to thank the Minnesota Historical Society Press for having faith in me to tell this story. The press staff, and especially editor in chief Ann Regan, led me through the nuances of publication with grace and patience.

Collaborating with Curt Brown on the manuscript of this book has been a great pleasure and a learning experience. Curt is an experienced newspaperman, historian, and author. I greatly appreciate his skill and contributions that make my scratchings more readable.

I sincerely appreciate the beautiful contributions of the six fine photographers whose images of the lighthouse are featured in this book: Christian Dalbec, Nathan Klok, Nicholas J. Narog, Dennis O'Hara, Hayes Scriven, and Paul Sundberg.

I would like to express my everlasting appreciation to the Minnesota Historical Society for giving me the opportunity to be a part of the Split Rock Lighthouse story. I will forever be grateful for the faith, trust, and support this great institution showed. I will never forget the many dedicated and talented people I worked with at Split Rock over the years. They always showed the lighthouse and the historical society in their best light.

And above all, I want to express gratitude and appreciation to my wife, Jane. Her optimism and willingness to share in this hectic yet remote life with humor and compassion made the years pass far too quickly. Thanks also to our children, John and Anna: the joy they brought us was immeasurable. They will have their own stories to share of growing up at Split Rock. It is humbling to think that we lived a happy family life at Split Rock for one-third of the total life span of the light station. We will forever be intertwined in the lives of the many families who made their homes in those three lightkeeper's dwellings on top of that cliff.

This book is a brief record of a time, a place, and a life that was filled with history and beauty. I hope that some of my great appreciation for the opportunity to live it comes through in these pages.

— LEE RADZAK

~~~

HEARTFELT THANKS to Lee Radzak for allowing us all to join his family on Minnesota's most spectacular cliff top. From his embrace of history to his eye for nature, I couldn't ask for a better lead partner for this project. Thanks to Josh Leventhal for bringing us together.

The view from Split Rock wouldn't be nearly as clear without Ann Regan's deft skill of organizing words and photographs. And special thanks to Adele Brown, my personal beacon, cutting through my fog for the last forty years.

— CURT BROWN